John St. Loe Strachey

Industrial and Social Life and the Empire

John St. Loe Strachey

Industrial and Social Life and the Empire

ISBN/EAN: 9783743306684

Manufactured in Europe, USA, Canada, Australia, Japa

Cover: Foto ©ninafisch / pixelio.de

Manufactured and distributed by brebook publishing software (www.brebook.com)

John St. Loe Strachey

Industrial and Social Life and the Empire

HOUSES OF PARLIAMENT

Photo. F. Frith and Co., Reigate.

Frontispiece

THE ... AND THE STATE

PART II

... AL AND ...
AND ...
THE EMP...

BY

... LOE STRAC...

London
MACMILLAN AND CO.
AND NEW YORK
1895

CONTENTS

PART I

INDUSTRIAL AND SOCIAL LIFE AND DUTIES

I. INDUSTRIAL AND SOCIAL LIFE

CHAP.	PAGE
1. Our Duty to our Country—Making the best of Ourselves	3
2. National Wealth	6
3. The Duty of Saving	10

II. THE GREAT INDUSTRIES

4. The Growth of National Industries—Changes caused by Machinery	13
5. The Saving of Labour	18

III. ASSOCIATIONS OF WORKERS

6. Trade Unions	24
7. The Objects and Organisation of Trade Unions	27
8. The Moral Advantages of Trade Unions—Strikes	31

CHAP.		PAGE
9. Capital	. . . . .	36
10. Increase in the Efficiency of Labour	. .	42
11. The Duty of Trade Unions	. . .	45
12. The Unemployed—Dangers of Trade Unionism	.	49
13. Trade Disputes—Boards of Conciliation and Arbitration	. . . . .	51
14. Capital and Labour	.	56

IV. Co-operative Societies

15. Co-operation and Division of Profits	. .	60
16. Growth of Co-operation	. . . .	63
17. Productive Co-operation	. . . .	67
18. Co-operators and Education—The Rochdale Pioneers	71
19. Other Forms of Co-operation—Its Advantages	.	76

V. Friendly Societies

20. Mutual Benefits	. . . .	80
21. Friendly Societies—Good and Bad	. .	82
22. Affiliated Societies	. . . .	86

VI. The State and Labour

23. The State and Labour	. . . . .	93
24. State Interference—The Factory Acts	.	96
25. The Dangers of Interference	. . .	100
26. The Health and Safety of the Worker—The Labour Department	. . . . .	103
27. The Government and Municipalities as Employers	.	106
28. The Duty of Workers	. . . .	109
29. Just Legislation and Impartial administration	113

CONTENTS. vii

PART II

THE BRITISH EMPIRE

I. THE EMPIRE

CHAP.		PAGE
1. THE DOUBLE DUTY OF A BRITISH CITIZEN—THE EMPIRE AND ITS DIVISIONS	. . . .	119
2. GREATER BRITAIN—COLONIAL INDEPENDENCE	.	123
3. THE VALUE OF THE COMMON CITIZENSHIP.	. .	129
4. IMPERIAL CO-OPERATION	. . . .	132

II. THE SELF-GOVERNING COLONIES

5. CANADA—NEWFOUNDLAND .	. .	139
6. AUSTRALIA	. .	146
7. SOUTH AFRICA	. .	155

III. CROWN COLONIES

8. CROWN COLONIES (1)	. .	. .	161
9. ,, ,, (2)	. .	. .	166

IV. PROTECTORATES

0. PROTECTORATES	. .	. . .	171

V. INDIA

1. INDIA (1)	. . . . . .	176
2. ,, (2) .	. . .	186

CHAP.
13. INDIA (3)
14. ,, (4)
15. ,, (5)

VI. CONCLUSION

16. OUR DUTY TO THE EMPIRE
17. THE UNITED STATES

APPENDICES

A. THE FACTORY ACTS
B. THE LABOUR DEPARTMENT MEMORANDUM
C. THE ROLL-CALL OF THE BRITISH EMPIRE

PART I

INDUSTRIAL AND SOCIAL LIFE AND DUTIES

I.—INDUSTRIAL AND SOCIAL LIFE

Chapter I

1. **Our Duty to our Country.**—No one can doubt that it is the duty of men and women to think not of their own interests, but of the interests of those who are dependent upon them; that is, of the interests of their families. But our country is only the great family to which we all belong. Men and women, then, should remember that it is their duty to think of the interests of their country, and should put those interests above all others. We must not imagine, however, that by caring about our country and thinking what is best for it, we shall run any risk of neglecting the interests of our families or of ourselves. If we rightly understand our duty to ourselves and our families, and do that duty, we shall at the same time be doing our duty to the mother of us all,—our country.

2. When Nelson spoke to the sailors of the English fleet just before a great battle, the words he used were: "England expects every man to do his duty." The words are just as true for the ordinary world, and for the common everyday battle of life in which we all have

to fight. Our country expects every man to do his duty whether he lives in England, Scotland, Wales, or Ireland. But in the interests of his country, of his family, and of himself, a man's first duty is to make the best of himself—that is, to make the best use of the powers of body and powers of mind with which he is born, and of the opportunities for using those powers which come in his way.

3. **Making the Best of Ourselves.**—It is easy to see that if men and women are to make the best of themselves, they must begin when they are boys and girls to plan how they shall do it. The first and most important way of making the best of ourselves is doing the work that suits us best. As we have all to work in some way or other, it is of great importance that we should work at what we can do well. Who can say that a man who is a born driver, and who can do anything he likes with horses, is making the best of himself if he becomes a clerk, and does nothing but add up figures or copy letters all day? He would be much better employed on a farm than in an office.

4. Again, a man with strong arms, and with the knack of swinging the hammer straight, will be doing much better for himself and for all of us if he becomes a blacksmith than if he becomes a tailor. There are two plain reasons for this. In the first place, the man who does the work he is fitted for does it easily and well; while the man who does work for which he is not fitted does it badly and with difficulty. But work we do easily and well makes us happy and contented.

5. The boy or girl then who takes care at the beginning of life to choose work which suits him or her

is far more likely to lead a happy and contented life than the boy or girl who takes no heed of such things. We do ourselves an injury by not choosing work that suits us.

6. Next, those who do work for which they are unfitted, instead of work for which they are fitted, injure their country. Any one can see that it is a great injury to a family if Mary, who is clever with her needle but bad at scrubbing, is set to scrub; if Jane, who is a good cook but poor at laundry work, is sent to do the washing; while William, who is a capital hand at minding the shop but a bad driver, is sent out with the van. It is just the same with the nation. If the children of the mother-land are all doing work for which they are not fitted, it will be bad for that great family the nation. It is then not only bad for the man himself, but bad for the country if he does work for which he is not fitted.

7. The duty of every boy and every girl at the beginning of life is, therefore, as far as possible, to choose suitable work. It is not, of course, always possible for a boy or girl, or man or woman, to get exactly the work which suits them best. In that case it is their duty to take what they can. No really worthy man or woman will stand idle because they cannot find the work they think suits them best. It is when they have a chance to do either what is suitable to them, or what is unsuitable, that they should be careful. It is at such times that foolish people begin to consider "Shall I find this work lighter, or more genteel, or more easy to shirk?" Instead, wise people ask, "Shall I make the best of myself at this work, or will that work suit me best?" Those who ask this and decide accordingly will be those

who will be doing their duty to themselves and their country.

3. *A born driver.* A man born with a capacity for driving.
4. *Knack.* A dexterous habit.

Chapter II

1. **National Wealth.**—What makes up national wealth—that is, the wealth of the nation as a whole, the total stock of wealth of all the people in the nation, rich or poor? To answer this we must first ask What is wealth? Wealth includes everything which men value, and for which they are willing to give something in exchange, such as food, clothes, houses, horses and carts. Thus, to take an example, a man's power to labour is wealth; for people will give money in exchange for it, and money is only tickets for so much food, clothing, and fire. We value money not for itself, but because we can at any moment exchange it for the thing we happen to want.

2. A man's cleverness is also wealth, because he can exchange it for money, and so for other things which are pleasant and useful. A wealthy nation is then one in which the people who make up the nation have a great many of the things which men value. But nations rightly desire to be wealthy, because when they are wealthy there are more of the things that men want to be distributed among the people. That is plain enough. If there are 1000 people, and if they are all to have clothes, food, coal and other things in plenty, there must be plenty of clothes, food,

Photo. F. Frith and Co., Reigate.

THE THAMES FROM LONDON BRIDGE

coal, etc., to be distributed among them. The more then there are of all these things the more each of the 1000 will be able to have of them. It is then the business of every man and woman in the nation to add something to the stock of things of all kinds wanted and used by the nation.

3. By working a person not only helps himself, but adds to the wealth of the nation, and so makes more to go round. The man who, by raising food out of the ground for men to eat, by spinning cotton for them to wear, or by writing books for them to read, increases the national wealth, does a useful action, and helps his country.

4. **Waste—a National Injury.**—On the other hand, men and women who waste the national wealth injure not only themselves but their country. It is for this reason that men and women should always try to put good work into whatever they are doing. It is the worst sort of waste to build a wall so badly that it will not stand, or to plough a field so that the crop put in will not grow properly.

5. When, then, we are tempted to do bad work either for ourselves or for other people we should refuse, and on the ground that to do so is to decrease the national wealth and to injure our country. No one, however, must suppose that because it is a good thing to increase the national wealth, that therefore it is the only thing we need think about. There are, of course, hundreds of other duties that come before it, and are far more important. At the same time it may help us all in our work to remember that by working well we do good not only to ourselves, but to our fellows.

6. Political Importance of the Question of National Wealth.—It is specially important when we are considering the making of laws to remember that it is our duty not to waste the national wealth. We should ask of our laws, new and old, "Will this law create a waste of the national wealth—that is, leave less of all the things men want to go round in the nation, and so make the poor poorer?" If the law would lead to a waste of the wealth of the nation we should be very careful how we agreed to it if it was a newly-proposed law, or how we let it remain a law if it was already one. Certain things have, no doubt, to be done by law which waste the national wealth, but we should only allow such laws when they can be shown to be absolutely necessary, and when, therefore, there is no other way out of the difficulty.

7. How to Increase the National Wealth.—It has been shown that every capable, industrious, and self-respecting citizen should do his best to add to the wealth of the nation. The way in which a man should try and add to the wealth of the nation is clear. He should make himself as good a workman as he can at the particular work he has taken in hand. This is to be done by acquiring and using skill and knowledge. There is no trade or calling so simple as to be impossible of improvement; and in most there are countless chances of doing whatever has to be done better than it was ever done before. A great many of the inventions which have done so much to make the world an easier place to live in were thought of by men determined to find out some new and better way of doing an old thing.

8. But to do things better and to make improve-

ments we must know all about what we are doing. The more a man knows about his trade or business the better he will succeed in it. If a blacksmith says, "I can work my hammer and anvil as well as my father, and shoe a horse as well as he could, and what more do you want?" it is pretty certain that he will never get the best possible work out of himself. If he says, on the other hand, "I mean to learn everything I can in books, or by talking to others, or by watching with my own eyes and reasoning in my own mind about the metals I use, and the best way of using them," we may be sure that this man will do something, perhaps a good deal, to improve his trade, and will get the best possible work out of himself.

7. *Calling.* Vocation in life.

Chapter III

1. How a Man Benefits by Skill and Knowledge. —A man who cultivates skill and knowledge in his own trade benefits himself and his country in three ways. To begin with, he is a happier man for so doing. The man who works without any thought of what he is about is like a slave or an animal, and has none of the pleasure which is gained by knowing how this effect springs from that cause, and how one thing depends upon another. Labour, when it is joined to intelligence and interest, is ennobling and makes men far happier than idleness. Labour, performed like a machine, and without knowledge, is deadening and stupefying. Next, he increases the national wealth, and so benefits both himself and his country. Lastly, his example helps to show others the advantage of applying skill and knowledge to the work in hand. Very few men are born without the power to acquire skill and knowledge. Those, then, who make no effort to gain skill and knowledge in some of their many forms deserve to be called the enemies of themselves and of their country.

2. **The Duty of Saving.**—There is another duty closely connected with the duty of making the best of ourselves and of our powers of work which must not be forgotten. It is the duty of saving—thrift. It is only by means of saving that the world has been able to move forward, and the lot of man to be improved. Savings are stores of food and clothes and firing put by for future use. It is true that people, as a rule, save in money, but that is the same thing as saving in food and clothes and firing, for pieces of money, as we have said, are only tickets which will any day buy these things. It is by means of savings that not only all the great undertakings, such as railways and canals are made, but that every trade and industry is partly carried on. They all require capital; but capital is only money saved up. Those then who save money, even if it is only a few shillings or a pound, add to the capital in the country, and make it easier for all sorts of work to be carried out.

3. There are hundreds of undertakings which would benefit the country and give employment to the labourer which cannot be carried out because enough capital cannot be found to set them going. The man, then, who saves money and invests it increases the

national capital—increases the chance of these beneficial works being executed.

4. **The Strength got by Saving.**—There is yet another reason, and a still stronger one, why every one who possibly can should save something. Even if he has provided against sickness and old age by belonging to a benefit society, a man should endeavour to put by some £10 or £20 in case of need. A man is not really a free man unless he has got such a sum saved and ready to live upon if things go wrong with him. If a man has no money put by, but has only what he can make from week to week, he is very often at the mercy of those that employ him. He may be obliged to take whatever wages are offered him. If, however, he has enough saved to keep him for six months the fear of losing his employment is not half so great.

5. A man with £20 in the bank can make a much better bargain when he sells his labour than can a man who, if he does not sell it at once, will be obliged to starve. The man, then, who wants to be really free and independent, and to discharge his social duties well and truly, should not rest till he has saved enough money to keep him and his family for at least six months. If the majority of workmen were in that position they would be far better able to make advantageous terms with their employers than they are at present.

4. *A benefit society.* See p. 80.

II.—THE GREAT INDUSTRIES

Chapter IV

1. **The National Industries.** — The great industries of the nation must always remain the same. To name them one has only to think of the chief needs of human beings. Men must always have food, clothing, fire, and houses; therefore the chief industries will be those that supply these wants. That is, first of all, agriculture—tilling the land to make it produce food. Next, the weaving and spinning of cloth, either from wool or cotton or other materials, to form clothes. Next, the working of coal to burn as fuel for cooking and warming. Next to that, the building of houses. As important are the industries on which these depend.

2. The industries just named cannot be properly carried on without all sorts of tools, and to make these tools iron and other metals are required. Getting metals, then, out of the earth must always be one of the greatest of industries. Another very great industry, though it does not actually produce anything new, is the industry of transport—that is, the industry of those who, either in ships, or trains, or in carriages, carts, and waggons, move goods and people from one place to another.

3. **Their Growth.** — Nothing is more remarkable than the way in which most of the great national industries have grown during the last fifty years. Take, for example, the cotton industry. In 1840 about 600,000,000 lbs. of raw cotton were imported into the United Kingdom to be made into yarn and cloth. In 1887 the amount of cotton used in the United Kingdom had risen to nearly 1,800,000,000 lbs., or about three times as much. Perhaps, however, the best way of showing the growth of the cotton trade is to point to the fact that, at the present moment, half the spindles in the world spinning cotton are at work in England. A quarter of these 40,000,000 spindles are at work in the town of Oldham, in Lancashire. Therefore, in the comparatively small English town of Oldham is spun an eighth of all the cotton spun in the world.

4. The woollen trade has grown almost as fast as the cotton trade, and is at this moment very many times greater than it was fifty years ago. In both cases many more men are employed now than formerly. It is the same with the coal and iron industries, and, indeed, with every industry in the country except one —agriculture, that is, farming. Practically the number of men employed on the land at the present day is about the same as it was fifty years ago. The reason for this is not difficult to find. The land fifty years ago was producing almost as much as it could in the way of corn and meat and vegetables, and, therefore, there was little or no room for an increase. It is possible, however, that by paying still more attention to the work of cultivation the land may be made to produce even larger crops than it does at present.

5. The growth of the manufacturing industries in England can be clearly shown by considering the number of people now employed in them, and comparing these figures with those of fifty years ago. In 1841 there were about 3,137,000 [1] persons engaged in manufacture. There are now about 7,300,000; and this increase is not merely due to the increase of population. In 1841 the population was 15,800,000. It is now (1891) 29,000,000. Thus the number of persons engaged in manufacture has more than doubled, while the total population has not quite doubled. The manufacturing population was a fifth of the whole in 1841. It is now nearly one-fourth.

6. **Changes caused by Machinery.**—One of the most remarkable things about the growth of the manufacturing industries in England is the increase of the use of machinery. Hundreds of things which fifty years ago were done by hand are now done by machinery. Still more important is the fact that the machines have been so greatly improved that they often do ten times the work they did, and do it better. Again, it must be remembered that machinery has been so much simplified that, in many cases, a man can now mind three or four machines where once he could only mind one. In all the great industries machinery has taken the place of hand-labour. It might have been supposed that this would have inflicted a great injury on the working classes, and that the use of machinery would have driven them from employment.

---

[1] These figures are given in Mulhall, *Dictionary of Statistics*, edition of 1893.

STEAM TURN-ROUND PLOUGH (JOHN FOWLER AND CO., LIMITED, LEEDS)

7. This was indeed the feeling with which our fathers and grandfathers regarded the introduction of machinery. When they saw a machine brought into use which, with one man to tend it, would do the work of twenty men, at, say, the cost of the labour of five, they concluded that in the future nineteen men would be thrown permanently out of work, and that this process would go on throughout the country till the only men employed in the work of manufacture would be a few tenders of steam spinners and weavers. Yet, as a matter of fact, the very opposite has happened. As we have seen above, there are more, not less, men employed in manufacturing than formerly; and the great increase in the use of labour-saving machinery which has marked the last fifty years has made the demand for labour grow even faster than the population. Instead of more machinery meaning fewer men, it has meant more men.

3. *Raw cotton.* Cotton as yet unmanufactured.

Chapter V

1. **Why Machinery does not Diminish Employment.**—How does it happen that this has been the result of labour-saving machinery? The answer is simpler than it looks at first sight. If 1000 yards of cloth are wanted and no more, and if twenty men were at one time required to produce them, then it is clear that the introduction of a machine which does the work of twenty men when tended by one must throw nineteen men out of employment. As a matter

LONDON AND NORTH-WESTERN TRAIN

of fact, however, it is never true that a fixed quantity of anything and no more is wanted. Only 1000 yards of cloth may be wanted while cloth is at a certain price, but directly that price is greatly reduced hundreds more yards are wanted. The world in reality will always want as much of the chief things of life as can possibly be produced by the people who live in it.

2. When, then, a labour-saving machine is produced what happens is this. The cloth, or whatever it may be, becomes cheaper, and more is taken and used than before, and so more is needed to be manufactured. Soon, then, we get twenty machines at work turning out cloth with twenty men to tend them. Our nineteen men are thus back at work again though in a different way. Sometimes, however, the process is not quite so simple as this; and not all, but only a part of the men displaced by the improved machinery find new work in connection with the new system of manufacture. When say only ten men get re-employed owing to the demand for more cotton, it may for a time seem as if the other nine were sure to be injured. Yet this is seldom really the case. The reason is this. If by introducing machinery you cheapen the cost of making cloth, and so sell cloth cheaper, the people who used to spend £1 a year on cloth in the future have only to spend say 16s. to get the same amount. But this means they have each year 4s., or say a penny a week, over to spend on other things.

3. **Nimble Sixpences.** — Some part of this 4s. they perhaps spend on more cloth, but the rest they will spend on other things, such as boots, linen, and hats. But spending more on boots, linen, and hats means that more of these things have to

be made, and the making of more of these things means that more men are employed. In other words, the shillings set free by cheaper cloth go at once to give more employment in other trades. Sometimes, no doubt, it is difficult to trace these nimble sixpences and shillings, but that it is true that the use of labour-saving machinery never injures the workman, but instead improves his condition, can be proved by the figures we have given above. Since the greatly increased use of machinery the number of persons employed in manufacture has, as we have said above, increased and not decreased, and increased not merely in numbers, but in proportion to the population.

4. **An Impossible Exception.**—Perhaps, however, it will be said how about cases in which the machinery which displaces the men does not create any saving, and produces not cheaper cloth, but cloth exactly at the same price? In that case the nineteen men who are thrown out of work will be able to get no work either in the cloth trade or elsewhere, for there will be no increased demand on the part of the public. The answer is, that such cases do not occur in practice. No manufacturer goes to the risk, expense, and worry of putting in new machinery unless he can see his way to a decrease in the cost of production. If the new machinery will not enable him to produce cheaper than he did before, he will not, take the trade as a whole, care to introduce it.

5. **Labour Saving and the Accumulation of Wealth.**—Save, then, in a few exceptional cases, and during the time necessary for things to settle down to the changed conditions, the introduction of labour-saving machinery invariably does good to the working

classes and to the country as a whole. It increases the wealth of the country, and so makes more to go round. *Nothing that does that can be of harm to the nation.* There never was, in truth, a more absurd statement than that of the poet who talked of the land

"Where wealth accumulates and men decay."

6. The land where wealth accumulates is the land where men do not decay. The land where they decay is the land where wealth is squandered and wasted, and not accumulated to assist in making provision for the future, or to keep those who are engaged in useful and necessary work, but not immediately capable of yielding things needful for human existence. Take, for example, the building of a great railway. It takes, say, seven years to build, and during that time yields nothing; but after those seven years it is an untold blessing to humanity. But if wealth had not been accumulated it could never have been built. We should then never forget that whatever increases the wealth of the nation is a benefit to the nation, and especially to those who are poor, and, therefore, deserves to be encouraged; and further, that whatever wastes the wealth of the nation is an injury to the nation, and ought to be put an end to as quickly as possible.

6. *Squandered.* Spent foolishly.

III.—ASSOCIATIONS OF WORKERS

Chapter VI

1. **Associations of Workers.**—Many of those who are engaged in trying to make the best possible use of their powers find that they can gain great and lasting advantages by joining together and forming what are called Associations. A man who stands alone in the battle of life is constantly at the mercy of evil circumstances of various kinds. By joining with others, and agreeing to stand or fall with them in certain of the relations of life, he gains a great deal of power. For example, ten men agree that whichever of them falls ill during their lives shall be helped by the other nine. Here it is clear that a great advantage is gained by combining, and that the men in the combination are in a much better position than are those who do not belong to it and stand apart and by themselves. If they fall ill they have no one to support them. This is, of course, only one example of combination.

2. There are plenty of other ways in which men can agree together to help each other. They can join to help and support each other to get good wages and good treatment in regard to working hours and other

matters. Such combinations are called Trade Unions. Next, they can combine either to make or to sell to themselves all the things one needs for daily life. These combinations are called Co-operative Societies. Next, they can join to provide against sickness and death, and to insure themselves a supply of money in old age. These associations are called Friendly Societies. Each of these ways of combining must be considered separately.

3. **Trade Unions.**—Those societies, associations, combinations or unions (the words all mean the same) formed among the workers to enable them to sell their labour to the best advantage are chiefly useful to persons engaged in working for wages. As has been noted above, they enable the labourer or the artisan to claim his fair share in the settlement of the conditions under which he is to labour. Often, too, they do more than that. They afford him support in sickness and old age, they pay for his burial and for that of his wife, and they give him help when out of work. Hence it happens that in almost all the industries and callings of the country Trade Unions have been formed.

4. **The History of Trade Unions.**—Trade Unions, such as we know them at present, have only existed for about a hundred years; but throughout the past we find traces of workers joining together to help each other, and to obtain better conditions for labour. The arrangement is one much too rational and obvious to have remained undiscovered till modern times. When at the beginning of the present century the working men began to form Unions on the existing model they met with strong opposition from the Government and

from Parliament. It was supposed that the Unions encouraged lawlessness, and that if allowed their own way they would destroy the trade of the country. No doubt the Unions of that time, to some extent, encouraged people to take this view. Their members occasionally indulged in great violence of language, and threatened that they would do things which were tyrannical and oppressive.

5. If, however, Parliament had been wise it would have paid little attention to such wild talk, but would have recognised the fact that men, as long as they do no violence to others, have a perfect right to try to improve their own position. That Parliament failed to see a truth which now sounds so simple was due to a mixture of ignorance and panic. Parliament was ignorant of the real state of the facts, because at that time the working classes had little or no voice in electing it. It was panic-stricken because of the violence of the workmen who, a hundred years ago, were ill-educated, though through no fault of their own, and were also full of prejudices and of hatred against those richer than themselves. The result was that combinations of workmen to get an increase of wages were forbidden, and that those who attempted to form them were cruelly persecuted.

6. Gradually, however, Parliament saw that it had made a mistake, and little by little the laws interfering with the right of combination were done away with. At last the right of combination was entirely and openly acknowledged, and by an Act of Parliament passed in 1875 Trade Unions were allowed full liberty of action, provided, of course, they did not use criminal means to support their action. The

result was to take away from the Trade Unions the last vestiges of any inclination towards lawlessness, and to make them what they are, combinations to enable working men to sell their labour to the best advantage.

4. *Rational.* Reasonable.
6. *Vestiges.* Traces; remains.
   Criminal means. Actions of such a kind that their performance would be a crime.

Chapter VII

1. **The Objects of the Trade Unions.** — At present the objects[1] with which Trade Unions are formed are—(1) To secure to the members of the Union the best return for their labour—that is, to obtain for them as high wages and as short hours as possible, and to see that certain restrictions as to the conditions under which they work are enforced; (2) To provide mutual assurance for the members by means of assistance in money in case of "sickness, accident, death, out of work, superannuation when disabled by old age, loss of tools by fire or other accident, and sometimes emigration."

2. **Organisation of Trade Unions.**—It is clear that to obtain these objects a great deal of organisation is required. No body of men can succeed in what they desire merely by coming together and expressing their wishes. They must make arrangements for carrying

[1] See *Conflicts of Capital and Labour*, by George Howell. Macmillan and Co.

out those wishes. These arrangements are called creating an Executive—that is, a smaller body for executing or putting into operation what the larger body agrees upon. The executive of a Trade Union generally consists of a committee or council elected by the whole of the members. Sometimes the election is for three months, sometimes for a year. Besides this council there are four chief officers—the president, the vice-president, the secretary, and the treasurer, who are also elected by all the members. This is the simplest form of organisation.

3. In most cases, however, the Unions are broken up into lodges or branches, and each lodge, since to a certain extent it manages its own affairs, not only helps to appoint a committee and officers for the whole body, but also appoints a committee and officers for itself. Thus all the important Unions have both a central and a local organisation. There are a central council and a central president, vice-president, secretary, and treasurer for the whole body, and there are also local councils and local officers for the branches. In the same way, just as there is a local general meeting of all the members of a branch or lodge, so there is a central general meeting of delegates elected by all the branches.

4. Next, there is a special set of officers called trustees, to whom the funds of the Union are entrusted. All the money belonging to the Union is banked in their name. They hold all the investments, and are answerable for their safe custody. Thus no money can be withdrawn without the knowledge and sanction of the trustees. Finally, there is a body of auditors, both in the branches and in the

central organisation, chosen by the members of the Union from among themselves, whose special duty it is to look into all the accounts, and to see that no money has been wasted or spent on things not authorised by the members.

5. Those officers whose duties do not take up all or any great part of their time work for their Union for nothing, or for some very small sum; but those whose whole time and energies have to be given have, of course, to be regularly paid. As a rule the general secretary is the only officer in a Union in this position. It must not be supposed, however, that he finds the post a very lucrative one. There are only two Unions in which the salary of secretary is £4 a week, and in most cases it is only £3. This is not high pay considering the character of the work done. Take it all round, the Trade Union officials are among the most underpaid men in the kingdom. It is very greatly to their credit that they should give so much devotion to their arduous work for so small an amount of remuneration. Those who talk of the Trade Union officials being highly-paid agitators are talking misleading and mischievous nonsense.

6. **The Work done by Trade Unions.**—To realise what is actually accomplished by Trade Unions, and to understand how they work out in detail the objects for which they are called into existence, it is best to take an instance, and see how the money is spent. A good example of a Trade Union is "The Amalgamated Society of Carpenters and Joiners," since it is that of a trade which is practised in every part of the country and known to all. This Union takes from each member a contribution of 1s. a week. In return

for this the member obtains a weekly "sick benefit" while he is ill of 12s. for the first 26 weeks, and 6s. a week afterwards so long as he is ill. His widow gets £12 on his death, and he on her death obtains £5. On being injured or disabled he gets a sum of from £100 to £50, and he is entitled to a weekly superannuation benefit of from 8s. to 7s. per week. When out of work he can claim 10s. a week for 12 weeks, and 6s. for another 12 weeks.

7. Again, in case of loss of tools by fire or other accident the member can claim the "out-of-work benefit." Lastly, in the case of a strike agreed upon by the Union the member obtains from 15s. to 7s. 6d. per week. This list of benefits will show how the workman by combination can secure himself against misfortune. The man who does not belong to a Union is at the mercy of circumstances, and cannot, if he gets too low an offer of wages, afford to wait for a better. The man who belongs to a Union can, on the other hand, to a great extent defy fortune, and is not obliged to take the first offer of work that comes his way. He can wait till a reasonable wage is secured him. Some Trade Unions are so organised that their members get no sick benefits or payments on death, and are merely combinations in which the men agree to stand together in regard to wages. These are, however, clearly not so beneficial to the men who belong to them as the Unions which are also benefit societies. In these the men stand together and help each other in all the risks of life. In the societies which give no benefits the men merely try to help each other in the one object—the raising of wages.

1. *Superannuation.* The condition of being so old as to be past work.
4. *Sanction.* Permission.
5. *Lucrative.* Profitable.

Chapter VIII

1. **Moral Advantages.**—It is clear that the ordinary workman gains a great many material advantages by belonging to a Trade Union. If he uses his Union in a proper spirit he may, in addition, gain a great many moral advantages. In the first place, membership of a Union teaches him the great lesson of working with other men, and of subordinating self-interest to the interests of the community. This is the lesson which we all need to learn in regard to our country, which is, after all, but a greater union. The artisan in his lodge sees that, if men are to live and work together without confusion and disorder, they must act according to fixed laws, that they must be patient and helpful, and that they must always keep before them as their supreme and final aim the general good. But this, only on a larger scale, is exactly the attitude of the true patriot.

2. Again, the obedience enforced in regard to the rules of the Union teaches the members the necessity for obeying the laws. Then, too, the knowledge that if the obligations in regard to the payment of the weekly subscription to the Union are not fulfilled, and if the member breaks his contract with the rest of the members and gets into arrears, he will have to leave the Union, and will be forced to go without the various

benefits he would otherwise have enjoyed, cannot but produce a great effect on a man's mind. It shows him the necessity of standing by his agreements, and the punishment which rightly falls on those who do not keep to their bargains. In this way the Trade Unions may act as schools, in which the members can learn how to do their duty as good citizens, and to accept that discipline without which the desire to do one's duty and to be a good citizen is useless.

3. **Dangers of Trade Unions.**—Trade Unions, like all other human institutions and like men themselves, have elements of evil in them as well as elements of good. And, just as in men, if these evil elements are not recognised and fought against, they may master the good ones and make the whole tendency of the Union bad instead of harmless. The first and worst of these evil tendencies is that towards tyranny and oppression. When a man feels very strongly the wisdom or necessity of a certain step, and when he considers that his own interests will be damaged by his fellows not taking that step, he is very apt to try and force them to take it, and to overcome any unwillingness by oppression and violence. But this is as true of a thousand men acting together as of one.

4. Hence Trade Unions are sometimes tempted to use violent means for getting what they desire. For example, they naturally wish to get all the workmen in a trade to join the Union, and they occasionally press the non-union workmen to join them in a way which is unfair and tyrannical. When they do this they commit a great moral wrong. Every man, as long as he obeys the law, has a right to choose what voluntary obligations he will undertake—to choose,

that is, whether he will or not belong to a Trade Union. To force him to join by threats of violence or by intimidation in any other form is a criminal act, and one which is not only punished by the Courts of Justice, but condemned by all good men. It must not be supposed, however, that all or any large portion of the Trade Unionists favour acts of coercion in order to make men join their societies.

5. **Violent Methods.**—The true Trade Unionist is entirely opposed to any such methods. In the same way, there is a danger that in the excitement of a strike the Unionist may be tempted to use violence to prevent persons who do not choose to strike from remaining at work. Acts of coercion of this sort are, no doubt, always disavowed by the leaders of the Unions, and usually quite sincerely, but the ordinary members of the Unions when on strike are, it is to be feared, often led away into violence. No one, of course, has any right to object to their trying peaceful persuasion on the non-strikers. It is when they overstep this line that they are to be condemned. Every man, then, who joins a Trade Union should make up his mind that, however great the temptation, he will refuse to help in any attempt either to force unwilling men into the Union, or to employ violent and oppressive means to prevent non-strikers from remaining at work when the Union men are on strike.

6. **Strikes.**—Trade Unions are frequently in danger of being led into acts which are both injurious to their members and to the country as a whole in their management of strikes. A strike or a lock-out is the stopping of work in a particular trade, or at a

particular manufactory, because the workmen and those who employ them cannot agree as to wages or hours of labour. Strikes can be no more condemned in the abstract than any other effort of men to get the best price they can for their labour. They are either wise or foolish according to the circumstances. No one says that an actor is wrong because he refuses the terms of the manager at an inferior theatre, but waits till a better salary is offered him. It may be the very wisest thing he can do. So no one has a right to blame a body of workmen who ask for a certain wage, and believing that they can get it refuse to take less.

7. **Ill-considered Strikes.**—What is unwise is not a strike, but a strike entered upon without due consideration. Hence there rests upon the Trade Union leaders a very great responsibility in the matter of ordering strikes. They are quite right, nay, it is their duty to their fellow-workmen to get as good pay and as short hours as possible, but in doing so they must be careful not to kill the goose that lays the golden eggs. It is all very well to get higher wages, but it is no good to get wages which are higher than the employer can afford to pay, and which, if insisted upon, will ruin his works and oblige them to be shut up. Those, then, who order strikes must consider not merely whether they have the actual power to make the manufacturer either grant higher wages or accept ruin, but to consider whether the employer or manufacturer can afford to pay more in wages.

8. **The Conditions under which Wages can be Raised.**—Whether the manufacturer can afford to pay

more wages depends upon a variety of circumstances. If the money paid to labour is increased the loss to the manufacturer must be made up in one of three ways. Either the amount paid to capital must be decreased, or else the price charged for the things manufactured must be increased, or else by the use of newer and better machinery, or by more careful superintendence and economy, the same number of men must be made to produce more. That is, in the case, say of a boot factory, if the men are to get higher wages, and the factory is to go on, either (1) the profits must be reduced and less paid for the capital required in the business; (2) the price of boots must be increased; or (3) the way of working be so much improved that the boots will not cost more to make than they did before in spite of the fact that the men who make them are better paid.

9. Unless the employer can in one of these three ways make good the loss he suffers by an increase in wages he will have to close his factory. He will not care, and indeed will not be able except perhaps for a comparatively short time, and as a temporary measure, to keep his business going. Before, then, the leaders of the men take the grave step of striking for an increase of wages they must consider whether it will be possible for the employer to do what they ask. It is worth while to notice more in detail the things which they have to consider under each of these heads.

1. *Subordinating.* Placing beneath."
5. *Coercion.* Compulsion.

Chapter IX

1. **Capital.**—In considering whether more money can be paid in wages by paying less to capital the men must remember what capital is. Capital is simply wealth accumulated in the form of money, and applied to industry. The man who buys a saw, and saws timber with it, is using capital to help labour. The man who builds a great factory and fills it with machinery is only doing the very same thing on a large scale. But capital, the necessary helper of labour, has its price just as labour has, and in the long run the price of capital, as of all other things, depends upon how much there is of it to be hired or sold, and how many people there are who want to hire or to buy it.

2. We talk of paying five per cent interest on capital; but this is only another way of saying that we hire capital, agreeing to pay rent for it at the rate of five pounds a year for every £100 hired. But as every one knows no one can start a factory of any kind without capital, which he either hires from himself or from some third person. Now the amount of hire or rent which a man wanting to set up, say a boot factory, is willing to give for other people's capital, or at which he will invest his own, depends upon what can be got for capital elsewhere.

3. **The Wages of Capital.**—If people can get a rent of five per cent elsewhere for their capital they will not lend to him at four; and he himself, if he can get five elsewhere, will not put money into the factory if he thinks that the profits will

not rise above four per cent. It would be better in such a case not to start a factory, but to hire his money out elsewhere at five per cent. In the same way, if a man has his money already invested in a factory, and the factory only pays him, say $2\frac{1}{2}$ per cent, while he can get five in other businesses, he will take the first opportunity he can find for shutting up his factory and taking out his capital. No doubt this is sometimes so difficult an operation that he will be unable to manage it, but we may depend upon it that if the capital in any business is for long being paid below the market rate the business will not prosper.

4. **When Capital is not properly paid Businesses do not prosper.**—To begin with, every year new capital is wanted for improved machinery, and for new processes, and for making good wear and tear and losses by accident. But if this new capital is not to be properly paid, it will be found that it will not come into the business. But the workmen in any trade have a direct interest in attracting as much capital as possible into the trade. And for this reason. The more capital comes into the bootmaking trade the more business is started. But the more businesses that are started the more demand there is for the labour of the bootmakers. This is easy to see. If there are ten boot-manufacturing businesses in a town the demand for labour will be brisker and wages better than if there are only five, for the pay of labour is raised by competition among the employers.

5. **The Necessary Question.**—Those, then, who are considering whether it will be wise to strike must ask the question—Is capital in the particular trade in which the strike is contemplated being

paid more than capital elsewhere? If the answer is Yes, then on this ground it may be safe to strike for an amount of pay which will not bring what is paid to capital below the rent of capital elsewhere. If, however, the answer is No, and it can be shown that capital, under all the circumstances, is not getting more than its market price, then those intending to strike must on this ground, at any rate, give up the idea of striking. To strike for higher wages if the increased cost is to come out of the payment made to capital when that payment is already only at, or perhaps below the market price, would be most foolish, and would end in driving capital out of the trade. But driving capital out of a trade is the very last thing which the men want to do. It means driving away that which increases the price of labour.

6. **Increase of Price.**—If the men have come to the conclusion that an increase of wages cannot be got out of the money paid to capital, they must next consider whether it can be paid by an increase in the price of the manufactured article. Take the case of a boot factory, at which the boots have hitherto been sold at 5s. a pair. Will it be possible for the boot manufacturer to raise the price, say to 6s. and pay the increase in his wages' bill out of the extra shilling? The answer depends upon many things. Certainly he will not, if other factories go on selling the same class of boots at 5s. per pair. Suppose, however, that the rise in wages would affect all the English factories equally, and that, therefore, if the price of boots was raised it would affect all England. In that case the thing might be done, except for one

EXTERIOR OF A BOOT FACTORY (MANFIELD AND SONS, NORTHAMPTON)

or both of two things. In the first place foreign boots might come in at 5s. per pair. In that case it would be impossible for the price of English boots of the same quality to be raised. They would simply cease to sell if their price were raised to 6s. The leaders of the men have, then, to consider what is the lowest price at which foreign boots can be sold in England, and to remember that the price cannot be raised above that without killing the English boot trade. But even when this has been considered and settled there is yet another matter to be taken into account. Will the raising of the price of boots, even if kept below the price of the foreign boots, make people use fewer boots in the year, and so injure the manufacturers and cause less work for the workmen?

7. **Increase in Price means Decrease in Demand.** —There is no doubt that a marked rise in price at once causes a decreased demand, even in apparent necessaries. Say that boots doubled in price. At once people would buy fewer boots; fewer boots would be ordered to be made, and the men in the boot factories would have either to do less work a week and take less wages, or else a portion of them would have to be turned off altogether. But neither of these things would suit the workmen. Unless, then, there is little or no foreign competition in a trade, and unless also the increase in price is not large enough to matter much, it cannot be to the interests of the workmen to obtain a rise in wages by a rise in the price of the manufactured article. In other words, the workmen must not rely upon the manufacturer being able to grant a demand for more wages by

A BOOT FACTORY INTERIOR (MANFIELD AND SONS, NORTHAMPTON)

raising his prices unless they have looked very carefully into the question of foreign competition, and of the ability of the market to bear an increase of price.

8. Fortunately all these matters are now very closely investigated by the officials of the Trade Unions before they agree to a strike. The offices of the Unions are usually well stored with trade statistics, and an honest endeavour is made by the men to find out whether the manufacturer can yield to their demands without having his business ruined.

8. *Investigated.* Looked into ; examined.

Chapter X

1. **An Increase in the Efficiency of Labour.**—In cases where an increase in wages can be obtained neither out of the profits given to capital nor out of an increase in the price of the manufactured article, it may still be obtained by increasing the efficiency of labour. Suppose the demand of the workmen in the boot factory would mean an extra £50,000 a year spent by the manufacturer; suppose, too, that at the same time it can be shown that either by introducing machinery, which will work quicker or use less coal, or by an increase in the working power of the individual labourer, owing to his being made stronger and more vigorous by the better conditions of life which come with better pay, or, again, by the stopping of some waste which has hitherto been overlooked, or by the use of less costly but yet as useful material, or finally,

by a combination of all these ways, £50,000 can be saved. Under those circumstances the manufacturer can grant the increase in wages without touching the remuneration of capital or the selling price. Can labour be made more efficient? is then a question for the Union leaders.

2. **The Problem for the Men.**—Lastly, Union leaders have to consider whether the money needed for more wages cannot be raised in all these ways—some from one and some from the others. Capital may be made to take a little less pay; prices may be raised a little, and the efficiency of the machinery and of labour—that is, the work done by each labourer—may be increased. The way just sketched is in fact the way in which the matter is considered and argued out by the leaders of a well-organised trade. As a rule, a well-thought-out and reasonable demand is not often refused by the masters. They soon see that the increase if not given voluntarily, can be wrung from them by a strike.

3. When, then, they do not in the long run yield to a demand for an increase in wages, it is pretty certain that they consider that it would not pay them to carry on business under the weight of a larger wages' bill. No doubt they are often wrong, for they are liable to be honestly mistaken in their calculations, just as are the officials of the Union, but as a rule, if a strike actually takes place it is a sign that the employer does not believe that he can find the money out of which to raise the men's wages.

4. **High Wages and Efficiency.**—A word must be said as to the effect of high wages on the efficiency of labour. It has often been noticed that higher wages

have by themselves, and without any extra improvement in machinery or any new stoppage of waste, increased and so cheapened production. The reason is simple. The badly paid man cannot afford to get enough food, to hire a good enough house, and to take enough rest to be in a condition to do work up to his full powers. Hence to pay him better—that is, to give him more food, more rest, and a better and healthier house—is often as much to the interest of the employer as of the employed. Of course there is a limit to this.

5. A manufacturer who tried giving his men £20 a day would soon find himself a bankrupt. Till, however, enough wages are paid to enable an ordinarily sober and thrifty man to live well and happily, and to cultivate both mind and body properly, the manufacturer will not be able to obtain really efficient labour. Unfortunately, no strict rule can possibly be laid down as to what is enough wages to enable a man to do the greatest amount of work of which he is capable. This amount can only be roughly arrived at after many experiments and trials.

6. **Hours of Labour and Efficiency.**—In the same way, short hours of labour have not unfrequently proved quite as productive as long ones. A man has only so much work in him each day. This work can often be done as efficiently in eight or nine hours as in twelve. The object, then, is to find out what is the amount of time which the average man requires for performing his daily capacity for work. Beyond that it is useless to keep him at work. He will only be spreading thin what ought to be spread thick, and either occupying the factory while another shift might be at work, or else keeping it open when it might be

closed, and the various expenses which always continue while a factory is open are going on. It is, however, very difficult to find out what is the least amount of time in which a man can spend his daily store of labour. Obviously, it must differ very much in different trades. A man may be able to attend to a steam engine and keep it oiled for ten hours a day, while another who works in a smithy may be utterly exhausted in six hours.

7. Again, there are factories which would not pay if only opened for eight hours, owing to the large part played in them by machinery. A machine may not be able to be made to pay unless it can be run for more than eight hours. In the case of hours then, as of wages, a very great number of things have to be considered, and the Union leaders who advise a strike for shorter hours are under a great responsibility. Unless they have satisfied themselves that shorter hours will not decrease the production and so increase the price of the thing produced, they are probably injuring the workmen by advising a strike.

1. *Remuneration.* Payment in reward of services rendered.

Chapter XI

1. **The Duty of the Trade Unions.**—The duty of the Trade Unions in regard to strikes is then perfectly clear. It is their duty to obtain as high wages and as short hours as possible for their members, and they have a perfect right to use the power of striking to gain

either or both of these objects. They must, however, always ask themselves before they order a strike, Will our demands, if agreed to, increase the cost of production as a whole? If they will, then the strike is unwise, and will in the end prove a failure. If they will not, owing to it being possible to induce capital to take less profits, or to render labour more efficient, or to increase the selling price, then the strike can succeed, and is not unwise.

2. **Trade cannot thrive when the Cost of Production Increases.**—No trade can thrive when the cost of production in the trade rises. But unless the trade thrives the labour attached to the trade will not thrive. Shall we by striking increase the cost of production in the trade permanently and really, and not merely apparently and for the moment, That is the question which the Trade Union leaders must be always asking themselves. After all, the men are partners with the masters, and what they want is not to injure the trade, but merely to get a different division of the total profits. To increase, then, the cost of production and so to kill the demand first, for the thing produced, and then for the labour of the producers, must in every case be an injury to the workmen who form the Trade Unions.

3. **Trade Unions and High Wages.**—It is the object of a Trade Union not merely to raise the wages of the men at work at any particular time, but to find work for all the members of the Union. Hence, if a Trade Union forces wages so high that a good many factories have to stop altogether, they make it impossible for a good many workers to find work at all. But these out-of-works have to be

supported by the Union. It is not then to the interest of the Union to raise wages beyond the point which can be borne by the whole body of manufacturers. When, however, from any cause there are a great many men out of work in a trade, the Union is sometimes tempted to try to get them work by suggesting that the factories shall work less hours.

4. Then, they argue, the unemployed will be able to get work. "The manufacturers," they say, "will want to produce as many boots as before. If then, we, the existing workers, work less and so turn out less, they will take on more hands and so bring in the out-of-works." This is sound enough unless the men at work expect the old rate of wages for less work. In that case they are asking for more wages —not perhaps for themselves, but more wages altogether.

5. Take an example. Suppose a factory in which 1000 men are employed, and that each man produces at the rate of eight pairs of boots a week.[1] There are, however, many unemployed in the town, and the Union officials suggest shorter hours in order to help them. Accordingly the factory is to work six hours instead of eight. But if the output is to be maintained this will mean that more than 333 extra men will have to be taken on—1333 men at six hours roughly equals 1000 men at eight hours. But suppose, also, that the bootmakers'

---

[1] These figures are not those of any existing factory, nor are they intended to be near those of an actual case. I have merely taken for the purposes of argument the figures which will work out plainest. They are simply intended as a model, and any one can fit on to the model the facts and figures of a factory that may be known to him.

wages during the time they worked for eight hours were £1 a week; then till the hours were reduced and the extra men were taken on, the weekly wages paid were £1000 a week. But in all probability this sum was all the manufacturer could afford to pay in wages in order to produce 8000 pairs of boots per week. If he could have afforded to give more the Union would have already compelled him to give more.

6. He will not, then, when he has to employ 1333 men instead of 1000 to turn out 8000 pairs of boots per week, be able to pay £1333 a week, or each of them £1 a week. Instead, he will have to say that he must reduce the weekly wages of his men to the point which will keep his weekly wages' bill for 8000 pairs of boots to £1000—that is, he will only be able to pay the 1333 men who work for six hours a day 15s. per week each. Shorter hours, then, when adopted to find work for the unemployed, and not because it is clear that as much or more can be done in them than in long ones, must mean shorter wages for those already employed.

7. The only apparent exception to this would be the case in which the wages being paid were in reality too low, and capable of being raised. Then, of course, instead of a rise three or four hundred new men might be brought into the factory, the total wage increased, and the hours worked decreased without ruining the factory. Such exceptions are, however, so rare that they need not be very closely considered. As a general rule, working short hours to bring the unemployed in a trade into work must mean either lower wages or ruin the trade.

4. *Sound.* Reasonable.
5. *Output.* The total quantity of manufactured stuff produced by a factory or mill.

Chapter XII

1. **Is it good to work Short Hours and get Short Wages in order to find Employment for the Unemployed?**—No doubt, under certain circumstances, it might be a good thing for the country as a whole that there should be a reduction of hours and of wages in order to give more employment. In other words, that the amount of money available for wages in a particular trade in respect of a particular amount of output should be distributed not among 1000 men, but among, say, 1333. The question depends mainly upon the amount of wages being earned by the employed at the time when the demand is made for shorter hours and shorter pay in order to admit the unemployed. If they are getting so large a wage that the necessary reduction will not bring the wage below what is sufficient for the worker to live healthily and happily, then the dilution of labour by bringing in the men out of work is for the public good.

2. If, however, the reduction would bring those already in work below that standard, then it is not for the good of the country that the unemployed should be brought in. It would be far better that they should either take to some other form of work or emigrate, or even be supported by the State as a whole. Anything is better than that the majority of workers in a trade should work under conditions as

to pay which will not allow them to make the best of themselves. That is certain to be an injury to the nation.

3. **The Dangers of Trade Unionism.** — Two dangers of Trade Unions deserve to be noticed. One is to be found in the attempt to limit the number of members in a Union, and so to keep the privileges of the Union as a monopoly for a few privileged workers. Another is the endeavour to use the Trade Union organisation not for trade objects, but for some political purpose. The first of these is a danger which has tended from time to time to threaten Trade Unionism. Fortunately, the Unions, as a rule, see that it is most unfair to restrict the number of members in a Union, and adopt the plan of making the entrance to the Society easy to all men of good character.

4. Every now and then, however, the spectacle has been witnessed of Unions trying first to prevent any men going to work who are not Union men, and then endeavouring to keep down the numbers in the Union. These two acts constitute a system of gross tyranny and oppression, and should be denounced and condemned wherever they occur by all honest and fair-dealing men. They have never been sanctioned by the wisest advocates of Trade Unionism, and the most successful societies have always acted on the opposite policy to that of restricting the number of their members.

5. The use of the Trade Union organisation for objects other than those connected with the bettering of the conditions of labour must always be a grave injury to the labourer. Fortunately, this was early realised by the Trade Union leaders, and they have up till now

steadily refused to identify themselves with either of the two great political parties. It is to be hoped that they will continue this policy, and will not lend themselves to the schemes of the politicians. Those schemes may be right or wrong, but it is clearly not to the interest of the Trade Unions to advocate them.

6. It is their duty to think solely of how they can obtain the best price for the labour of their members, and how they can generally improve and secure their position in regard to the share of production which should belong to labour. If they keep firmly and resolutely to these objects they will do good work for their members. If, however, they allow their attention to be taken off by this or that set of political schemes their power of helping the workers will dwindle and be destroyed.

3. *Monopoly.* An advantage in the possession of a few people only.
5. *The two great political parties.* See *Representative Government*, chapter xxxiii, Macmillan and Co.

Chapter XIII

1. **Trade Disputes.**—In the course of business, disputes between employers and employed, not only as regards wages, but in connection with all sorts of minor matters, are likely to arise. In former days these were as often as not settled by strikes, and the work of production was again and again interrupted

by sudden stoppages of work. As Mr. Burt[1] has said, petty strikes in the collieries of Durham and Northumberland were, forty years ago, of almost daily occurrence. Fortunately, the good sense of both the owners and the workmen has been used to devise a remedy, and arrangements have been made by which the greater number of trade disputes are now settled without a strike, either by boards of conciliation, or else by arbitration.

2. **Boards of Conciliation.**—In most of the great trades there exist Boards of Conciliation or Joint-Committees formed of equal numbers of representatives of the employers and of the employed to whom are referred all disputes. Very often, however, the secretary of the Trade Union, by talking the matter over with the employer can at once settle the question. Especially is this the case if the Trade Union is a large one, and if the workers in the factory where the dispute has arisen form but a small portion of the whole body of workers represented by the secretary.

3. In that case the secretary is in an exceedingly favourable position for knowing how far it would be wise to press the demands of the men, and how much he ought to yield. He is in full sympathy with the men, and has full knowledge of their views, and yet is not concerned with the petty quarrel of the moment. Best of all is the situation produced when the employers as well as the men are organised in a Union. In that case the secretaries of the two Unions can meet

---

[1] Mr. Burt, at present Under Secretary for the Board of Trade, is the trusted adviser of the Durham and Northumberland miners. He was one of the first working men to enter Parliament. He is universally respected for his honesty, moderation, and good sense.

and settle all minor disputes by negotiation, while more important matters can be referred by them to a standing joint-committee.[1] By this means strikes are avoided in all but extreme cases.

4. It might be supposed that Joint-Committees and Boards of Conciliation, since they have no legal power to enforce their awards, would be of little or no use. When the men on the one side and the employer on the other have come to a final decision, what, it is sometimes said, is the good of more talking. If two forces, it is argued, are contending in opposite directions, the weakest will have to give way. That sounds unanswerable. Yet, as a matter of fact, it is found that if the two sides can be got to meet, and to talk freely across a table about their differences, a way out of them can generally be discovered.

5. Till men have met with the distinct wish to find a method of conciliation they do not really know the exact dimensions of the dispute. No workman and no master, then, can be called wise if he ever condemns a Board of Conciliation as useless, and refuses to agree to one on the ground that it is impossible for him to yield further. However much either side is convinced that it has nothing to yield, it has no right to refuse to make an effort towards conciliation. Every dispute, until it has been settled, seems one in regard to which a settlement is impossible. Yet we know that in practice hundreds of disputes can be, and are settled by reason and plain speaking.

[1] A standing joint-committee is a committee composed half of representatives of the men and half of those of the masters.

6. **Arbitration.**—Closely allied to conciliation in trade disputes is Arbitration, which may indeed be described as the next step to conciliation. When the plan of talking over and settling a dispute in a joint-committee fails, it is often found possible to refer the matter to some impartial person, both sides agreeing to accept his decision whatever it may be. This person, called either the arbitrator or the umpire, hears the evidence on both sides, and then decides as he thinks just. Sometimes he acts alone, at others both sides choose six or seven men who sit with him and make up a Board of Arbitration. In that case the impartial man chosen from outside acts as chairman and has the casting vote.

7. It cannot, of course, be said quite so certainly as in the case of conciliation that employers and employed ought to agree to arbitration. There may be cases in which the employers or the employed will be obliged to say, "This is a case of life and death, and we simply dare not allow it to go to an arbitration—the result of which we pledge ourselves to abide by no matter what it may be." The employers may say, "An award unfavourable to us on this point must mean ruin;" or the employed may say, "An award against our claim would result in misery and starvation, and that we cannot risk." These extreme cases are, however, very rare. In ordinary cases it is clearly the duty of both sides to agree to arbitration, and so to avoid the waste and ruin of a strike. Unless and until all efforts to arrive at a peaceful settlement have been employed, the side which insists upon forcing on a strike or a lock-out is to be condemned, as acting contrary both to the best interests of the

Photo, H. T. Reed, Tottenham Court Road.

THE THAMES FROM TOWER BRIDGE

nation, and to the best interests of the trade in which the dispute occurs.

1. *Petty.* Small, insignificant.
2. *Conciliation.* The act of reconciling persons of opposite views.
4. *No legal power to enforce their awards.* No power to inflict punishment upon those who will not accept their awards.

Chapter XIV

1. **Capital and Labour.** — The Trade Union organisations have done a great and excellent work in educating their members in the matter of self-government, self-help, and self-respect. They may add to the benefits thus conferred by teaching the workers that capital and labour are partners in every trade, and that the work of production is not carried on by a conflict between them, but by their co-operation. Both are necessary elements in all production on a large scale. Let us look at the establishment of an industrial enterprise from both sides. The capitalist knows that he cannot produce unless he gets so many workers to act with him; but he cannot get these for nothing. He has, therefore, to consider what is the greatest amount he can afford to pay out of profits to secure these partners in the work of production.

2. Sometimes he can secure these partners at less than this maximum sum—in which case his own share of profits rises. Sometimes he can get them at this sum or something very near it. Sometimes, again, he cannot get them for the sum which he calculates to be the

greatest amount that can be paid to labour. In that case he does not start his industry, for he sees that it could not pay. If we look at the matter from the workmen's point of view the process is in reality much the same. If they are to get work in a new industry they must meet with capital which will enter into partnership with them. But to induce capital to come into partnership they must give it such a share of the profits of production as will pay it at least as well as it is paid elsewhere—that is, they must hire capital at a price which will induce it to enter into the partnership; for capital is worthy of its hire, and cannot be had for whistling.

3. It is then plain that both capital and labour are wanted to carry on the work of production—that both have a price, and that no offer below that price will make either of them agree to co-operate. If capital tries to beat down the price of labour too low, labour will not work, and the partnership cannot be formed. Again, if labour tries to beat down the price of capital too low, capital will not be forthcoming, and the partnership cannot be formed.

4. But in partnerships it is never found wise to make either partner take only the bare share of profits to which he is entitled. The wise capitalist accords to labour such a share of profit as will make the labourer contented and so efficient; and the wise workers see that it is to their advantage to let capital be well enough paid to be attracted to the particular trade. All this sounds simple enough, but unfortunately it is often not acted upon.

5. The workers, when they demand higher wages, are often not sufficiently careful to avoid frightening

away capital. They sometimes argue that capital in a particular trade once embarked cannot run away, and so may be squeezed to any extent. "It is tied by the leg, and we can therefore make any terms we choose. It must accept almost anything we like to give it." That would be all very well and true enough if a very important matter had not been forgotten. If when once an industry had been set going no more capital was wanted, the workers might be right to argue in this way. As a matter of fact, however, no industry can flourish or even be maintained in efficiency unless there is a constant flow of new capital into it. Not only does machinery have to be constantly repaired and renewed, but a whole new plant has to be set up every ten or twelve years.

6. But who is going to find this new capital if, in the trade in question, labour has behaved toward capital as if it were a prisoner, and has given it the harshest treatment? Capital only flows readily into those trades in which it is treated well. But, as has been pointed out, a steady flow of capital into a trade means a flourishing trade. But a flourishing trade means brisk employment for the workers. Hence it is madness for the workers to think that because a certain amount of capital seems tied to a trade they can use it just as they like. They can do nothing of the kind. Unless they make their trade attractive it will languish and decay, and they with it.

7. The very same thing is true of the capitalists. If capital tries to drive too hard a bargain with the workers by arguing, "They are committed to this trade, and know no other, and are therefore tied by the leg; hence we can treat them as we like," it

always injures itself. If the workers in a particular trade are squeezed unfairly they soon degenerate. The best men leave the trade, and no new ones who are good workmen flow into it, and the consequence is that the labour in the trade soon becomes bad and inefficient. It does not, and never can pay either capital to squeeze labour or labour to squeeze capital. Only when there is a fair partnership between them can trade flourish for the benefit of both.

2. *Maximum.* Highest, greatest.
5. *Plant.* The whole body of machinery in any particular factory.

IV.—CO-OPERATIVE SOCIETIES

CHAPTER XV

1. **Co-operative Societies.** — It has been shown how working men may help themselves by means of Trade Unions. Yet another form of associated self-help is to be found in what is called Co-operation, or working together for a common purpose. Co-operation may be applied to any of the things which men desire to do, but as a rule it is applied either to distributing or else to producing the things used in daily life, or to both. It will be readily understood that if men are to co-operate in such work as distributing, or making things, like food and clothing, they will have to be very closely and strictly organised. A hundred men could not manage a shop or a factory merely by agreeing to do so. They must form a permanent society, and be bound by well-understood rules and regulations.

2. Before, however, describing the manner in which the co-operative societies are, as a rule, organised, it will be as well to consider how the impulse towards co-operation ordinarily comes into being and how it works. Let us suppose that in a small town there are a hundred wage earners who are anxious to better

themselves, and to get the best possible results out of what they spend. They notice that everything they buy has to pass through a great many hands and to pay a great many profits, and they ask, Could not those profits be somehow secured for us, the consumers?

3. Their next step is to agree to club some of their savings together, and to see if they cannot make a saving by supplying themselves with groceries, food, and clothes. Accordingly, they start what is called a co-operative store. They form, that is, a small society, with a common fund, and out of this fund they buy, either from the makers or from the wholesale dealers, the boots and shoes, the cloth and the tea and sugar, which the members of the society need, and buy them, of course, at wholesale prices, which are very much lower than those of the retail trade.

4. Wholesale prices are so very much cheaper than retail for two reasons: First, the goods are bought in large quantities. But goods can always be sold cheaper in large quantities than in small. Secondly, the retail trader has not got to be paid his profit. No one can work for nothing; and, therefore, the man who keeps a retail shop is obliged to ask a price which will pay him for the trouble and expense of keeping shop. Now when the society has got its goods at wholesale prices it can do one of two things. It can either sell them to its members at wholesale prices, increased by just enough to cover the expenses of distributing the goods, or it can act as the shopman acts—can, that is, sell them at a price which will give a profit, and when that profit is made, divide it among the members of the society. Either plan is the system of co-operation applied to distribution.

5. Co-operation in Practice.—But though both forms of co-operation may be good in theory, it is found in practice that the Co-operative Stores which charge their members prices which ordinary shop-keepers charge, and divide the profits thus made every quarter, succeed the best. The reason is plain. It would be very difficult for Co-operative Stores to know what prices to charge for their goods if their object was really to sell as cheap as possible—that is, only to charge just enough above the wholesale market price to pay for the expenses of distribution. If ten men buy a 100 lbs. chest of tea from the merchant at £5, and each take a tenth, it is possible for them by paying a boy, say 10d., to take round the parcels to their houses to sell it to themselves at 1s. 1d. per lb. But when a hundred men are buying not only tea but a number of different articles in various quantities, these calculations cannot be satisfactorily made. Hence, as we have said, it is found very much better to charge ordinary prices and to make a division of the profits.[1]

6. Division of Profits.—How is the division of profits to be made? One plan would be to divide them equally among all the co-operators. Another, to divide them in proportion to the sums spent by

---

[1] The system of trading established by the so-called Co-operative Stores of the west end of London, such as the Army and Naval and Civil Service Stores, has been left out of consideration. These institutions—useful and well managed as they are—are not Co-operative Stores in the true sense of the term, but rather great trading concerns based on the principles of ready money and cheap prices. They do not differ from the great shops of the kind organised in London by Mr. Whitely or Mr. John Barker, except in the fact that purchasers must be members. The profits are divided, not among the purchasers, but among a small body of shareholders.

each member on purchases. This, on a moment's reflection, will be seen to be the fairer plan. Under it those who support the Store most benefit most. As a matter of fact, however, the division of profits is not quite so simple as this. No Co-operative Store, however small, can be carried on without capital. This capital is found by the members. But naturally they do not care to lend it to the Store for nothing. They expect it, when used in the Store, to give them as good a return as they could get elsewhere. Hence interest has to be paid on the capital thus lent.

7. In most, indeed, in practically all Co-operative Stores each member has to lend at least one pound of capital to the Store. He may lend more, but must not lend less. The first necessary charge on the profits of a Store, after the payment of working expenses, is, then, interest on capital, and after that a division in proportion to the sums spent on purchases by each member.[1]

Chapter XVI

1. **Other Conditions.**—It must not be forgotten that it is considered essential in almost all Co-operative Stores that members should pay ready money. This not only makes it impossible for the societies to have bad debts, but enables them to have plenty

---

[1] In most Co-operative Stores of the kind described non-members are allowed to purchase, but they only receive, as a rule, half the percentage paid on members' purchases. A fair arrangement, since any man can become a member.

of money in hand with which to make their wholesale purchases. If they gave credit to their members they would be obliged to borrow more capital, and so pay more interest, and so have less profits to divide on purchases. No Co-operative Store that does not require ready money can succeed. Another fact may be mentioned. Though a member must have at least one £1 share in the Co-operative Society to which he belongs, it is not necessary that he should pay that £1 down at once. He may become a member by authorising the Society to stop his share of profits paid in the form of a percentage on purchases till his £1 per share is fully paid up. In this way a man need not wait till he has obtained £1 to become a member of a co-operative society, but becomes a member the day on which he makes his first purchase.

2. **Co-operative Societies as Savings Banks.**—It must not be supposed that the only advantages gained by charging ordinary prices, and then dividing profits in proportion to purchases, are those of convenience. Co-operators claim that besides this, their system of conducting business enables them (1) to avoid a form of competition with the shopkeepers, which might be considered unfair by the latter; and (2) to act as savings banks for their members. The advantage of this arrangement can easily be seen. If the Co-operative Societies sold their goods at as low prices as possible members would in all probability only be tempted to take larger quantities—to take five ounces of tobacco instead of a quarter of a pound, and not to put by the price of an ounce. Again, if they got their tea a halfpenny a pound cheaper, that halfpenny would in all probability not be saved. It may

be good economy, but it is very difficult to save in small sums.

3. The Co-operative Society, however, performs this difficult task for its members. The halfpennies are all taken care of, and by the end of the quarter make a very good show. When at the end of the quarter a working-man is told that he has got £2 standing to his credit, he feels that he has done better than if he had got all his necessaries a little cheaper. What shall he do with that £2 ? If he had it in his hand he might very likely spend it. But it is not in his hand, but in the Store.

4. In all probability, then, he decides to let it remain there, and to receive interest on it as capital. But if he does this every quarter for twenty years, as thousands of co-operators have done, he gets to be the owner of £100 of capital almost without knowing it. If his society had simply sold him groceries and clothes and boots cheap, it is very unlikely that he would have saved a quarter of that sum. In this way Co-operative Stores have a right to claim that they are savings banks as well as retail traders.

5. **The Growth of Co-operation.** — Though co-operation began by retail trading, it soon grew and expanded into other branches of industry. At first the Co-operative Stores started in various parts of England dealt, like ordinary shops, with the nearest wholesale dealers. Soon, however, the co-operators began to ask whether they could not apply the principle of co-operation to wholesale as well as to retail trading. If, they argued, a group of families can agree to form a Retail Store, why should not a group of Retail Stores agree to form a Wholesale Store

and buy straight from the manufacturer and the importer? Accordingly, two such Stores, called "Wholesale Societies," one for England and one for Scotland, have been formed, and the principle of dividing profits according to the amount of purchases has been applied to them—that is, the Retail Store, like the member, shares in the profits of the Wholesale in proportion to its purchases.[1]

6. But the principle of co-operation did not stop even here. After the Wholesale Societies had been formed the committees of co-operators who managed them began to ask, "Why should not the Wholesale, instead of buying the things it needs from manufacturers and importers, manufacture and import for itself? We are asked every month for so many hundred pairs of boots and suits of clothes, and for so many chests of tea. Why, instead of buying them from third parties, should we not employ shoemakers and tailors to produce for us the shoes and clothes; and in the case

---

[1] *Co-operative Statistics.*—How great has been the use made by the working men of England and Scotland of the principle of co-operation is shown by the following figures:—There are at present over 1460 Distributive or Retail Stores in Great Britain. Their sales amount to £32,000,000 a year, and their capital is about £12,000,000. The two Wholesale Societies do a business in proportion. The sales of the English Wholesale are about £9,000,000 a year, and of the Scottish about £3,000,000. In addition, there are about 150 manufacturing or productive societies, and eight federal corn-mills. The corn-mills do a business of about £2,000,000 a year, and the other productive societies of about £1,000,000. Thus the total annual sales of the Co-operative Societies of Great Britain are about £46,500,000. It is further calculated that during the last thirty years the business done has reached £560,000,000, and that of this £48,000,000 have been profits distributed among the working classes. These figures show how great is the power of self-help contained in the principle of co-operation.

of the tea and tobacco and rice, etc., why should we not charter ships to carry them for us?" As a result, the Wholesales took to manufacturing and importing direct, and at the present moment the Wholesale Societies are very large manufacturers and merchants.

> 6. *Charter.* Hire at an agreed price. The legal document signed on such occasions by the owner of the ship on the one side and the person who hires the ship on the other is known as a *Charter party.*

Chapter XVII

1. **Productive Co-operation.**—It has been shown how by a series of steps the retail co-operators have become producers. It must not be supposed, however, that when production is carried on by a Wholesale Co-operative Society it is necessarily co-operative production. When the Wholesale sets men to work making shoes, it acts exactly like any other employer, and pays weekly wages for work done. Co-operative production is something quite different. Take the case of a hundred men who are engaged in a cloth mill.

2. They work for wages, but have no rights of ownership in the mill. One day, however, some of them put their heads together and argue thus: "Suppose we hundred operatives were able each to put down ten pounds and so to make up £1000 capital. With it we might buy a small mill and be able to set up on our own account. In that case the profits derived from our skill and labour would go

into our pockets. We should, in fact, be our own masters, and should share the profits that now go into the employer's pocket."

3. In a considerable number of cases this, or something not unlike it, has been accomplished by the workers in particular factories. These factories, then, are instances of productive co-operation, while those belonging to the Wholesale Societies are rather factories owned and worked by consuming co-operators. As to which end of the chain that binds the consumer and producer it is best for the principle of co-operation to be applied, there has been much dispute, but into this dispute we cannot enter at length.

4. We will only note that some co-operators declare that the Wholesale Societies ought to apply the principle of profit sharing to all the work done by them, while others declare this to be so difficult as to be virtually impossible, and consider that men who co-operate as consumers have a right to think mainly of the interests of the consumer. In all probability it will be found that there is room for both systems of co-operation. It is a great mistake to suppose that improvement in human affairs can be accomplished by one, and one means only. The poet Tennyson spoke well when he said that

> "God fulfils himself in many ways,
> Lest one good custom should corrupt the world."

5. Co-operators sometimes dream that in time every one will be a co-operator, and that the days of individual trading will be entirely done away with. That, however, is not likely to happen, nor should it per-

haps be desired. This "one good custom" might corrupt the world if it were the only one, and might take away from men their independence and energy.

6. **Co-operation and the Retail Shops.** — It is often said that the Retail Co-operative Stores compete unfairly with the retail shops, and that they have inflicted a great injury on many worthy men who, but for them, would have been able to earn an honest living. A little reflection will, however, show that this is by no means a fair accusation. Since the true Co-operative Stores only sell at the ordinary prices, and do not attempt to *undersell*, their competition is not a bit more dangerous than that of other shopkeepers. Since any one who likes may open a general shop, the shopkeepers in a particular town are no worse off from the competition of the Co-operative Stores than they are from that of an independent tradesman who shows more push and enterprise than they do. In practice this is well recognised, though not perhaps in theory.

7. What the small shopkeeper dreads is the invasion, not of a Co-operative Store, but of one of the big shops with low prices, an attractive front of expensive plate-glass, and an immense choice of articles. There need not be any real fear that the Co-operative Store will destroy the retail shop. Both fill a want, and both can flourish. And in one particular the Co-operative Store has done and can do the shopkeeper a good turn. It can teach him the inestimable value of ready money to trading. It is bad debts far more than competition by Co-operative Stores that injure the retail trader.

8. **The Moral Principles professed by Co-operators.**—It would not be fair to deal with co-

operation and neglect the great efforts made by the more intelligent among the co-operators not to divorce moral considerations from trade, and to keep a high standard always before their members. We all agree that it is the duty of the individual man in private life to obey certain moral laws. The co-operators wisely declare that a man cannot escape from the duty of obeying these moral laws by associating himself with other men. They bind the association as they bind the men who make it up. Accordingly, co-operators have steadily condemned the notion that, while men must individually be just and humane and considerate, they may, when associated in business, be unjust, cruel, and callous. In order to enforce their views on this point, the Union of co-operators—a body formed for mutual help and support out of the members of Stores scattered through the three Kingdoms—bind themselves in their associations to observe certain principles.

9. The first of these principles all honest men consciously keep before them in the conduct of their business undertakings. The other two if not generally acted on consciously, are often unconsciously followed, and with great advantage to the individual trader. The man who does not try to grasp at too big a profit, but makes a fair division of profit between the workmen he employs and the purchasers to whom he sells, ends by being far more successful than the man who makes both his employées and his customers discontented by asking from them the last possible penny.

10. **Advantage of the Introduction of Moral Considerations into Trading.**—That the co-operators

were wise in insisting upon the introduction of moral considerations into their work cannot be doubted for a moment. By doing so they have proved once again that it is absurd to say that moral considerations have no place in business. They have a place there as in every other department of human life.

> 8. *The Objects of the Co-operative Union.*—"This Union is formed to promote the practice of truthfulness, justice, and economy in production and exchange.
>
> "1. By the abolition of all false dealing, either (*a*) direct, by representing any article produced or sold to be other than what it is known to the producer or vendor to be, or (*b*) indirect, by concealing from the purchaser any fact known to the vendor, material to be known by the purchaser, to enable him to judge of the value of the article purchased :
>
> "2. By conciliating the conflicting interests of the capitalist, the worker, and the purchaser, through an equitable division amongst them of the fund commonly known as profit :
>
> "3. By preventing the waste of labour now caused by unregulated competition."

Callous. Heedless of the feelings of others.

Chapter XVIII

1. **Co-operators and Education.** — In order to prevent their societies becoming mere trading concerns the earlier co-operators insisted that a certain sum ought every year to be set aside for educational purposes. On the whole, this principle has been carried out with loyalty and perseverance, and though some societies show a more liberal spirit in this matter than others, there are few which altogether neglect the claims of

education. Co-operation, then, can claim to help the working man, not only in the matter of pounds, shillings, and pence, but in education and self-improvement.

2. **The History of Co-operation—The Rochdale Pioneers.**—The history of co-operation in England shows so clearly what may be done by those who

ROCHDALE CO-OPERATIVE STORE (OLD BUILDING)

determine to help themselves, that it is important to notice it in a certain amount of detail. The first Co-operative Store founded on what co-operators now regard as sound principles was that of the Rochdale Pioneers. In 1844 a band of twenty-eight flannel weavers at Rochdale resolved to try what associated effort could do towards bettering their position. Accordingly, out of their scanty wages, for wages were not then what they are now, they contributed at the rate of 2d. a week each till they had scraped together some £28 of capital. With this they opened their humble shop in Toad Lane, Rochdale.

3. But though their shop was humble their principles were anything but narrow or confined. Their ideal was to improve both themselves and the world in general, and by no means stopped at "getting things cheap." At the end of the chapter is the list of the objects which the Society adopted from the very beginning.

4. **The Store in Toad Lane.** — Contrast these objects with the account which Mr. Holyoake gives of the opening of the little store in Toad Lane on the night of 21st December 1844. Tidings of the new departure had spread in the town, and like all new departures it was unpopular, and attracted to it far more enemies than friends :—

5. "Many a curious eye was that day turned up Toad Lane looking for the appearance of the enemy; but, like other enemies of more historic renown, they were rather shy of appearing. A few of the co-operators had clandestinely assembled to witness their own *dénouement;* and there they stood in that dismal lower room of the warehouse like the conspirators under Guy Fawkes in the parliamentary cellar, talking on whom should devolve the temerity of taking down the shutters and displaying their humble preparations. One did not like to do it, another did not like to be seen in the shop.

6. "However, having gone so far, there was no choice but to go farther, and at length one bold fellow, utterly reckless of consequences, rushed at

the shutters, and in a few minutes Toad Lane was in a litter. On the night that our store was opened, the 'doffers' came out strong in Toad Lane, peeping with ridiculous impertinence round the corners, ventilating their opinions at the top of their voices, or standing before the door inspecting with pertinacious

ROCHDALE CO-OPERATIVE STORE (PRESENT BUILDING)

insolence the scanty arrangements of butter and oatmeal. At length they exclaimed in a chorus: 'Ay, the owd weavers' shop is open at last.'"

7. In all probability, if the " owd weavers " had not kept a high ideal before them their store might still be an insignificant grocer's shop. As it is, it is the

finest building in all Rochdale; and its illuminated clock is a symbol of what may be done by light and knowledge. It is true that the twenty-eight flannel weavers did not carry out all their objects. That is a common experience. Men seldom do all they would like. The important thing to remember is that they carried out some of them wisely and well, and that in all probability, if they had aimed lower, they would have done less rather than more.

3. *Ideal.* The scheme they put before themselves.
The Rochdale Pioneers. — "Their objects were to form arrangements for the pecuniary benefit and the improvement of the social and domestic condition of its members, by raising a sufficient amount of capital by shares of £1 each, to bring into operation the following plans and arrangements:—

"1. The establishment of a store for the sale of provisions, clothes, etc.:

"2. The building, purchasing, or erecting a number of houses, in which those members desiring to assist each other in improving their domestic and social condition may reside:

"3. To commence the manufacture of such articles as the society may determine upon, for the employment of such members as may be without employment, or who may be suffering in consequence of repeated reductions in their wages:

"4. As a further benefit and security, the members of the society shall purchase or rent *an estate or estates of land,* which shall be cultivated by the members who may be out of employment, or whose labour may be badly remunerated:

"5. That as soon as practicable the society shall proceed *to arrange the powers of production, distribution, education,* and *government,* or in other words, to establish a self-supporting home colony of united interests, and assist other societies in establishing such colonies."

6. *Clandestinely.*   Secretly.
   Dénouement.   The conclusion of their enterprise.
   Temerity.   Rashness.
   Pertinacious.   Persistent.
   Owd.   Old.

Chapter XIX

1. **Other Forms of Co-operation.** — Though co-operation has succeeded best in retail and wholesale trade, *i.e.* in distribution, or else in some simple form of production, the principle has been and is being applied to many other matters. For example, there is a Co-operative newspaper—*The Co-operator.* There is also a Co-operative Insurance Company, and Co-operation has been most successfully applied to house building. Attempts have been made to apply Co-operation to agriculture, but here, unfortunately, comparatively little success has been achieved. The fact is to be greatly regretted, as in theory it is difficult to point to any industry which is better suited to the application of Co-operation. Suppose ten labourers, each with savings of, say £15,[1] resolve to take a small farm, and use their £150 in stocking it, and then work it in their odd hours.

2. If the farm were worked so as to produce a portion of the various things which the ten men and their families need,—namely, milk, butter, meat, corn,

---

[1] It is said that labourers with £15 do not exist. They might easily do so, however, if they would put off marrying till twenty-five, or, still better, never spend more than one shilling a week on beer, spirits, and tobacco.

potatoes, cabbages, etc.,—and if the ten men were to agree to buy these necessaries from their farm, a market would be at once secured, and it is difficult to see why, granted that the work was loyally done, a beginning might not be made which would end as successfully as many of the retail experiments. Numbers of stores which now do business on a large scale were first started in the spare time of their founders. They opened shop after their daily work was done, and either attended to it in turn, or else paid some one to keep shop for an hour or two each evening. Agriculture offers so fair a field for co-operation that we cannot help thinking that sooner or later a successful attempt will be made to conquer the difficulties which seem at present to block the way.

3. **Co-operation and the Trade Unions.**—It must not be forgotten these two forms of self-help for workmen are by no means antagonistic. Indeed they may be said to be allies. This alliance was recognised by the following resolution, which was passed by the Trade Union Congress in 1883:—"The interests of our two movements are absolutely identical. Co-operation is essentially a labour movement; the flower of our workmen are its supporters, and many of our prominent unionists are among its trusted leaders. Year by year co-operation becomes a larger employer of labour. . . . It is undeniably a movement for the elevation of the working people. Duty and self-interest should therefore alike prompt the unionists of the country to do all they can to assist its progress and shape its policy by becoming its active coadjutors and associates."

4. **The Advantages of Co-operation.**—We have

shown how co-operation may benefit the working man by putting money into his pocket, and how the Co-operative Store, acting as a sort of "Self-acting Savings Bank," may turn him into a capitalist on a small scale. These, however, are by no means the only advantages drawn from co-operation. Its other advantages are equally important. In the first place, co-operation tends to prevent waste. But, as has been shown above, waste is the great enemy of the poor and of national wellbeing. Only by getting more to go round can the position of the poor be improved. But waste, instead of making more to go round, diminishes the amount available for distribution. But it may be asked, How does co-operation prevent waste? By doing away with unnecessary middlemen, and by bringing the producer and consumer closer together.

5. We have all seen a bucket after being filled at a pond passed down a line of men to the place where the water is wanted. That is what happens with all the articles of manufacture. But each one of the men who make up the line has to be paid for standing all day passing the bucket on. But if twenty men have to be paid to stand passing on the bucket when, as a matter of fact, five would be enough, there is a great deal of waste in employing the extra fifteen.

6. Co-operation often shows a way of decreasing the length of the line, and of making a short cut between the producer and the consumer. (1) Co-operation then stops waste. (2) It encourages good feeling and the sense of fellowship, making men realise that the good of the community as a whole, and not merely their own selfish aims, ought to be considered.

(3) Lastly, co-operation develops the intelligence of the co-operator, and gives him not only self-reliance, but business knowledge of a kind which is most useful when viewed from the standpoint of the interests of the State.

2. *Loyalty.* With faithful adherence to the principles proposed.

V.—FRIENDLY SOCIETIES

Chapter XX

1. **Mutual Benefits.**—Another form of association by which not only working men, but all members of the State, may help themselves, are Friendly Societies. We have noted how Trade Unions, besides helping the workman to dispose of his labour to the best advantage, and to protect his interests in the partnership into which he enters with the capitalist to carry on the various works of production, in most cases do something to provide against accidents, sickness, old age, and death. Friendly Societies are societies whose sole work is to help and befriend their members in such cases. They are formed among workmen of different trades, and have nothing to do with labour questions. Their object is simply to insure those who belong to them against the evils of accidents and sickness, and the inevitable occurrence of old age and death.

2. **The Principle of Organisation followed by the Friendly Societies.**—The principle on which the Friendly Societies act is both obvious and simple. Let us take the case of a hundred able-bodied men belonging to a town or village. These men, let us also suppose, are getting wages which

enable them to live in fair comfort, but which are not enough to make saving easy. What is to happen if any one of them is suddenly taken ill, and so unable to earn his wages, or if he grows too old to work, or, again, if he dies, what is to happen to his wife and children? The answer, in the case of the man who has not been able to save, must be a very terrible one.

3. How can these evils be avoided? By the hundred men agreeing together and saying, "We will each pay so much a week, say a shilling or sixpence, into a common fund, and this we will do as long as we live and are able to work. If, however, any one of us gets ill or meets with an accident he shall receive so much per week, as long as he is ill, out of the common fund made up from the weekly payments of those who are well. In the case of those who die a certain sum shall be handed over to the widow and children of the deceased. Lastly, those who live to an age after which they can no longer work shall receive an old-age pension of so much a week."

4. Here, then, we see what association can do. The man who does not enter the association is haunted by the thought, "If I meet with an accident or fall ill I shall starve, or be dependent on charity, or be forced to take poor relief. If I die there will not be even enough money to bury me. If I live till I am past work I shall be without any hope of help but the parish."

5. On the other hand, each one of the men who agree to stand together and help each other is able to say: "Not only am I secure while I am well enough and young enough to work. Even if ill-luck overtakes

me I shall not sink into hopeless misfortune. If I fall ill I shall get sick-pay till I am better. If I die there will be money to bury me and to help my wife at her hardest pinch, and if I grow too old to work I shall get an old-age allowance."

6. Working men have not been slow to see the benefits which are thus to be got from association, and, accordingly, a very great number of Friendly Societies have been started to do some, if not all, of the things we have mentioned as possible through association. Some of these societies belong to particular towns, districts, and villages, others again to the whole country. Altogether their members number over 10,000,000, and they hold funds to the amount of £90,000,000 sterling.

CHAPTER XXI

1. **Friendly Societies good and bad.**—Those who are anxious to obtain the benefits to be got from membership in a Friendly Society must not think that one Friendly Society is as good as another, and that it will be wise and prudent to join the first Friendly Society they hear of. Like everything else in this world, Friendly Societies are both good and bad, and, therefore, the greatest care should be taken to choose the good and avoid the bad. By a bad Friendly Society we mean a society which is so faultily constructed or so ill-managed that there is a great risk of it not being able to perform its promises to those who join it.

2. Think what this means. It has often happened

Photo. Elliott and Fry, London.

THOMAS BURT, M.P.

that a man has during the greater part of his life regularly paid his subscription to a Friendly Society in the hope of being able, in the case of illness, to get sick-pay. At last an accident makes it impossible for him to work any longer, and he applies for sick pay. Unfortunately, however, his Friendly Society was a bad one and has mismanaged its affairs, and the unfortunate member finds that it cannot pay the money due to him.

3. No greater disappointment than this can be imagined. To avoid it, men before they join a Friendly Society should inquire as to its rules and method of management, and should satisfy themselves as to its soundness. Nor must the member be content with merely finding out a good society at the beginning. When he has got into a sound society he should determine to do his part as a member to keep it sound. An institution, like a man, may begin good, but may by neglect become bad. Hence it is the duty of every member of a Friendly Society to watch its doings, and to do his best to stop foolish or unwise actions, if any such actions are contemplated. Only by such care and vigilance are human institutions kept from falling into bad ways.

4. **Bad Societies and how to know them.**—How is a man to know a bad society? One of the chief ways of knowing a bad Friendly Society is to notice whether the society promises more than it can perform. But how, it may be asked, can an outsider without knowledge and experience find this out? The answer is, by comparing the terms of the society with some well-known and firmly-established society like the Oddfellows or the Hearts of Oak.

5. If the Friendly Society about which inquiry is being made offers better terms—that is, offers to pay more sick-pay and more funeral money for a smaller subscription than do these great societies, it may almost certainly be concluded that it is promising more than it can perform, and that it should be avoided by prudent men. But even if its promises are fair and reasonable, and not too good to be true, the man who is thinking of joining should not stop his inquiries.

6. If possible, and especially if the society is a small one, he should find out something about the men who take the chief share in the management. If they do not seem to be men of honesty and worth he should not join. Lastly, he should in no case join a society which is not registered in the Government Office provided for that purpose, called "The Register of Friendly Societies" (28 Abingdon Street, London, S.W.). A society may be a bad one even though it is registered, but unless it is registered it is very unlikely to be satisfactory. Societies that are registered are not obliged to have perfect rules or to be well managed, but they are obliged to let their members know something of their management.

7. Again, in societies that are registered, the members have far more power to enforce good management if things seem to be going wrong. The duty of a man who joins a Friendly Society, and no man should refrain from joining one unless he feels that he can in some other and equally satisfactory way, such as by insuring with an insurance company, provide against sickness and death, is to inquire (1) whether the society he thinks of joining is registered; (2)

whether its terms are reasonable, and not of the kind which promise more than they can perform; (3) whether the committee and officers who manage the society are persons worthy of trust and confidence.

8. If these questions can be answered satisfactorily, let him join, but with the resolve that he will do his part in keeping the society from adopting dangerous and unsafe ways of managing its affairs, and from failing to carry out its obligations to its members.

9. **Model Rules.**—Model rules have been drawn up in order to guide those who want to form a Friendly Society, and may be obtained from the Registrar of Friendly Societies. No society which follows them will promise more than it can perform. It would not, of course, be fair to say that all societies which promise more are not trustworthy, but it may be safely said that the nearer their rules are to this model the safer they are.

7. *Enforce.* Compel.

CHAPTER XXII

1. **Various Forms of Friendly Societies.**—The work done by the Friendly Societies can be best made clear by the noting the various forms of Friendly Societies in practical operation. The first, the largest, and most growing class is the class of societies with branches, or Affiliated Orders, as they are more often called.

2. **Affiliated Orders.**—In these societies the branches largely manage their own affairs, but are

ODDFELLOWS' CERTIFICATE

under the control of a central body and possess a central fund. The Independent Order of Oddfellows (Manchester Unity), the Foresters and the Shepherds, and the Sons of Temperance are examples of these societies. The annual meetings or congresses of the branches are great features of these societies, and do much to educate and enlarge the views of the managing members. In all, there are now about 100 Affiliated Orders, with 20,000 branches, some 2,000,000 members, and funds amounting to £15,000,000. In an excellent account of the Friendly Societies, published in *Whitaker's Almanack* for 1894, it is noted, as a proof of the indirect benefits conferred by membership, how large a number of members of various affiliated orders have obtained positions of credit in our municipalities. These men found in the Friendly Society a school for civic life.

3. **The Oddfellows.**—One of the most important of the great Affiliated Orders is the Independent Order of Oddfellows. This society has over 700,000 members and a capital of about £8,000,000. Its annual revenue is over £1,250,000, and in 1892 it paid its members during illness and on death nearly £800,000. Its motto shows its principle of action. It is "Friendship, Love, and Truth." There are other great societies, which are nearly as large and proportionally quite as prosperous. The Order of Oddfellows is only named as an example of the size and importance of the great societies.

4. **General Societies.**—The second and next largest class is that of the *General Societies*, such as the Hearts of Oak, which, unlike the affiliated orders, have no convivial meetings, no lodges, and no secret

ceremonies, but are conducted on purely business principles. It has been pointed out (see *Whitaker's Almanack*) "that these societies labour under the disadvantage that their magnitude and the want of personal connection between the members expose them to the risk of frequent claims for sickness, and thus call for special vigilance from the managing officers." They have, however, advantages of their own which do not belong to the affiliated orders. They are, in fact, Mutual Insurance Companies.

5. **Sharing Societies.**—Another class is that of the Sharing or Dividing Societies. Here, as a rule, the common fund subscribed by the members to provide against death and sickness is divided at the end of every year, provision, however, being first made to meet all claims that may have arisen.

6. **Burial Societies.**—Certain societies confine themselves to providing for the burial of their members. These generally collect the instalments by means of collectors.

7. **Other Societies.**—There are, besides, some dozen other forms of Friendly Society, including the "County Societies," which were usually not self-established, but set on foot by means of outside help, and the "Village Clubs," which are the simplest and most primitive form of Friendly Society. Sometimes these village clubs are registered under the Act, but oftener they do not choose to go through the form, with the result that their funds are at the mercy of the men who are the office-bearers for the year.

8. **Building Societies.**—Building Societies, which are voluntary associations formed for the purpose of providing their members with freehold houses, hold a

sort of half-way position between the Co-operative and the Friendly Societies. When properly managed they are excellent institutions, and have done much good work in enabling men to become the owners of their own houses. On several occasions, however, mere trading speculations have masqueraded under the name of Building Societies, and have brought misery and ruin on the unfortunate men who joined them. All, then, that has been said in regard to the necessity for care and caution in choosing a Friendly Society may be repeated in regard to them. If a man will take the trouble to find out a good Building Society, and use it to get a house of his own, he will be doing much to secure his happiness and his independence. The man who lives in his own house, and can feel, that come what may, he will have a roof over his head, has secured himself against some of the worst evils of life.

9. **Value of Voluntary Associations.** — We have spoken above chiefly of the material value of voluntary associations, such as Trade Unions, Co-operative Societies, and Friendly Societies—that is, of their use in raising and improving the material condition of the workers. They have, however, a value beyond this. They act as schools for the education of the grown-up citizen. Nothing can be more important than that the affairs of the nation shall be well managed. But since every householder of full age has a vote, every householder has an equal duty to perform in regard to the work of government. It is his duty to consider what new laws should be made, and to choose wise and good men to make whatever changes may be necessary, to enforce the

laws already made, and to carry on and uphold the government of the country. This is an easy thing to write about or to speak about, but it is a difficult thing to do. And like all other difficult things, those who have practice in the matter and have learnt by experience will do better than those who have had neither experience nor practice.

10. Schools for Citizenship.—Nowhere can a man get better practice for doing his duty as a citizen, and for helping to manage the affairs of the State wisely and well, than in those voluntary associations of the workers—Trade Unions, Co-operative Stores, and Friendly Societies. If a man has learnt to act usefully and prudently in any of these societies he will know how to act usefully and prudently in the greater affairs of the country as a whole. The Duke of Wellington said that the battle of Waterloo was won in the playing fields of Eton. By this he meant that the men who had learnt self-command, self-reliance, courage, endurance, and the power of acting together while playing football and cricket, were able in after life to use those qualities in fighting their country's battles.

11. The same thing may be said, but still more strongly, of the voluntary associations. In them men may learn how to do their country service in the all-important work of Government. When the politicians propose a new law and the voter has to consider whether he will send to Parliament a member who will vote for or against that law, he can often test its wisdom by asking himself "How would a similar line of policy act in my union, or store, or society?" Again, his experience as an officer or a committee man

of his union, his store, or his club, will help him to judge men, will teach him the value of reason and moderation, and the uselessness of bluster, flattery, and humbug.

12. If he says to himself, "If a man talked like that in lodge I should know him to be a foolish, untrustworthy fellow," he has a standard by which to judge wild and random talk when it is indulged in by those who seek to manage the affairs of the State. Again, experience in managing the affairs of his society will teach him that when once you have chosen a good and capable man it is far better to treat him with confidence, and to trust him in details, than to be always trying to tie him down on this or that little matter. No good management will be got either of great or little affairs without trust being reposed in the man who manages. But nowhere better can these lessons be learnt than in lodge. Here, too, again may be learnt the great lesson that penny wise is often pound foolish. But nowhere is this principle truer than in national affairs.

2. *Municipalities.* The governing bodies of our great towns.
4. *Vigilance.* Care; watchfulness.
7. *Primitive.* Earliest.

VI.—THE STATE AND LABOUR

CHAPTER XXIII

1. **The State and Labour.**—We have seen how the workers are able to help themselves by associating among themselves. They can also be helped in certain ways by the action of the State—that is, by the laws, and by what is called the administration—*i.e.* the direct action of the Government. At first it might seem as if the State could and ought to do everything that a voluntary association of workers can do. People sometimes argue, " The State is simply a great association: why then should it not be as helpful and do as much for the worker as a Trade Union? Why not use its wealth and its power to do more thoroughly and more speedily what the Trade Unions try to do?" Such arguments are, however, based on a mistake, as a very little thought will show.

2. If the State were entirely made up, say of carpenters, the State could, no doubt, do for the people who formed it as much as and more, perhaps, than the Carpenters' Union does for its members. But then no State ever was, or ever will be made up of only one class of men. A State has in it men of all trades and

all professions, workers and non-workers, capitalists and non-capitalists. But since the State is a mixed association of this kind, and since justice and equality are the first principles of all association, the State cannot, as can a voluntary association, make laws to benefit a particular trade.

3. The State is an association which must think of the general benefit, that is, of the benefit of all its members, and not of any one class in particular. In olden times—the bad old days which, politically, we should neither regret nor imitate—the State often fell into the hands of a particular class, and this class used the power of the State—that is, the power of law-making—not for the general good, but in the interests of the ruling class. The result was bad government, injustice, and the creation of privileged classes. The men who happened for the moment to be strongest thought of themselves and their privileges rather than of the good of the nation as a whole. If, then, the workers were to use the laws to further their own special interests they would be falling into the evil ways of the privileged classes of olden times.

4. **The True Principle.**—The only true principle upon which the State can act is that of the general good. The carrying out of this principle does not, however, prevent the State doing things to help particular classes, provided that such help confers a general benefit, and takes place under exceptional circumstances. The principle merely demands that when such help is given, it shall be given because the condition of the class proposed to be helped makes it necessary in the public interest that something shall be done for it. For example, and to take an extreme

case, when it is found that men in a particular trade are being poisoned, or otherwise injured by the bad conditions under which they work, the State rightly makes a law to prevent employment taking place under such conditions. The general good demands that men, even if they are willing to do so, shall not be allowed to run unnecessary risks or to injure themselves irreparably in health. For it is for the general benefit, and for the good of the nation as a whole, that no class in the community shall by destroying its health produce weak men and women. The healthiness of the race is a matter of national concern.

5. **The Question of Degree.**—When the State is asked to do something to help a particular class it is necessary to ask, Will the interference of the State be for the general good? No hard and fast line can be laid down, but each case must be decided on its merits. There are, however, one or two general principles which ought to be remembered and taken into consideration whenever this demand is being considered. The first and most important of these is, that the State should forbid as few things as possible, and make as few things as possible criminal. In other words, it is for the general good that men should be left as free *as possible*. We say, as possible, because there are, of course, hundreds of things which men cannot be left free to do. Men cannot be allowed to kill and steal, and commit other crimes of violence. The old lawyers called these " things bad in themselves." Those which were less clearly wrong, such as driving on the wrong side of the road, or selling beer without a licence, they called " things bad because they are forbidden."

6. Now every one can see that the fewer there are

of these last the better. No man wants to have more chances of disobeying the law and getting punished than he can help, and he therefore says, "Only forbid the things which it is absolutely necessary to have forbidden; leave me free as regards other things to take my own choice." When, then, we come to a particular case of forbidding something by law, we have to consider which is the greater evil—to add another thing to the list of things forbidden, or to let some class or set of men and women run the risk of being injured or of injuring themselves. Another principle which ought to be borne in mind is expressed in the question, "Would the class which it is proposed to help by the new law be able to help themselves if the State did not interfere?" If they would, then it is clearly unnecessary to help them by law, for the law never does things so completely or so well as does voluntary effort.

Chapter XXIV

1. **State Interference in the Interests of Labour.** —In the United Kingdom there have been a great many instances of State interference in order to help the workers, but they have always been agreed to on the ground (1) that the general good of the nation demanded a remedy; (2) that in the particular case, adding to the list of things forbidden was a less evil than not interfering; (3) that the case was not one in which the people who were to be helped could help themselves. These, then, are the three great considerations which should guide us in regard to

State interference in regard to labour. By these we should try and test every demand for more State action.

2. **The Factory Acts.**—The greatest and most important example of State interference in the interests of labour is to be seen in what are called the Factory Acts.[1] About fifty years ago it was found that women and children were working in factories under conditions which were a disgrace to the nation. The hours worked were so excessive, and the sanitary condition of the factories so bad, that the health of the women workers was destroyed, and the children either died or grew up weak, stunted, and deformed. Accordingly it was determined to place the employment of women and children in factories under strict regulations. The younger children were forbidden to be employed at all; and the women and older children were only allowed to be employed for ten hours at a time, and with proper intervals for meals, and proper arrangements as to health.

3. Here was a clear case for the interference of the State. It could not but be for the general good to prevent such terrible injuries to the mothers of the population, and to children who, if allowed to be overworked, had no chance to grow up strong and healthy. No one can doubt that it was a far less evil to add to the list of forbidden things than to allow these horrors to continue. Lastly, it was clear that the women and children were not strong enough to help themselves, and if not helped by law would never be able to better their condition.

4. **Mines Acts.**—The same good reasons for the

[1] See Appendix A, p. 217.

State interfering with the conditions of labour prevailing in coal mines, produced the *Mines Acts*, under which labour in mines is strictly regulated. Fifty years ago women and young children were allowed to work in the mines. The results were even worse than in the factories before the Factory Acts. The women did the hardest and most unhealthy part of the work, and often with the most disastrous effects upon their health. In many cases they dragged the coal trucks through the passages of the mines. After a careful consideration of the whole subject, it was decided that work underground was not proper work for women, and that it tended to injure them morally and physically, and to unfit them for motherhood. Accordingly an Act was passed forbidding women to be employed underground. Further, the law insists that the mine owners shall use every reasonable precaution to ensure the safety and health of the men in their employ.

5. **Government Inspectors.** — It would obviously have been little good to pass the Factory Acts and Mines Acts, and not to have insisted on their application. That would be like enacting that public-houses should close at a particular hour, and then taking no thought as to whether they really did close at the hour required. Accordingly, a number of inspectors are appointed by Government, whose business it is to see that the Factory Acts and Mines Acts are properly carried out. These inspectors visit the factories and mines. In the factories they inquire whether women and children are employed for too long hours, whether any children under age are at work, and whether proper time is allowed for meals—an hour for dinner and half an hour for tea—and whether the sanitary state

Photo. F. Frith and Co., Reigate.

BRANDON COLLIERY

of the factories is satisfactory. In the case of mines they also see that the proper safeguards against explosions and poisonous gases are observed.

2. *Stunted.* With neither mind nor body properly developed.

Chapter XXV.

1. **Dangers of Interference.**—Though every one must admit that State interference was perfectly justified in the cases of the Factory Acts and the Mines Acts, no reasonable man or woman who looks into the subject will fail to agree that it would be very easy for the State to interfere too much, and that one result of such over-interference might be to injure rather than help those in whose supposed interests the interference was undertaken. The temptation to prevent women doing hard work is a very strong one, but it would not be at all wise to yield to it too easily. For instance, there are a great many kinds of hard work which no man quite likes to see a woman doing. When women are seen doing field labour, weeding or hoeing, and exposed to the weather, we feel inclined to say, "That is not women's work and ought not to be allowed."

2. Yet it would be a greater injury to these women to pass a law to forbid them to do field work than to let their backs be bent by toil and their faces bronzed by sun and rain. If we could add to a law forbidding field work to women, another law giving every woman ten shillings a week without working for it, well and good. But we cannot do that. Hence, if we were to

forbid a number of forms of work to women which they now use to earn their daily bread, we should be inflicting on them a grievous wrong. We should be forcing them to starve or to do worse.

3. No doubt in extreme cases, like forbidding women to work underground, the law did right. It would, however, be unwise to add other cases of prohibition without grave consideration. The more trades and occupations are forbidden to women by law, the greater the temptation to evil courses to which they are exposed. That would indeed be a terrible state of society, in which the fallen women could say, and say truly, "What other path did you leave open to me?"

4. Let the State deal with the extreme cases—the cases in which it can be said, "Almost anything is better than women being employed at such work." The ordinary instances of unsuitable work for women should be left to the instinct of chivalry in the men. Men should teach themselves to feel, "I have no right to let my wife, my daughter, or my sister (as the case may be) do such work as this, nor will I as long as I can use my hands or my brain." Such a spirit as that among the men is worth hundreds of Acts of Parliament or an army of inspectors.

5. **Children.**—The danger of State interference in the case of children is very much less. Children are the men and women that are to be, and the State ought to see that, while they are children, and unfit from want of knowledge and experience to look after themselves, they shall not be injured by overwork or by labour at unsuitable trades. Children, and especially young children, are somewhat in the position of slaves.

They must do what their parents bid them. But careless or wicked parents may force or allow their children to do work which will do them harm, and prevent them making the best of themselves in after life.

6. The State, then, has a right to step in and say, "You shall not injure the young plant; leave it alone till it is full grown." Of course even here it would be possible to overdo the interference, and to prevent the father and mother having a proper control over their children, but, as a rule, the State may more safely interfere in the case of children than of grown people. It is right that grown people should, as a rule, look to themselves for help and not to the State. Children, however, soon grow out of childhood, and till childhood is over should be wisely protected. The State, in fact, may rightly say to the careless parents, "We will not allow you to let your children do what no wise or kind father and mother will permit their children to do."

7. **Dangerous Employments.**—The manufacture of certain articles of commerce is attended with very considerable danger. These dangerous employments have been placed under special regulations, intended to make them as little dangerous as possible. This is perfectly reasonable. The laws of all civilised peoples forbid suicide—self-murder. But men who work at dangerous trades not in the safest ways, but, as often happens, under conditions which sooner or later are bound to bring about premature death, are really committing slow suicide.

8. The State is therefore quite justified in stopping men pursuing dangerous trades except under proper

safeguards. But it is found in practice that the most efficient way of enforcing these safeguards is to forbid the employers to employ men unless when using the best of them, and to make the masters responsible for carrying them out.

Chapter XXVI

1. The general Health and Safety of the Worker.—It may be said, " If it is right to protect women and children from working too long hours, and from working underground, to supervise the conditions of work in mines for miners, and to insist upon all possible safeguards being used in specially dangerous trades, why should not the State interfere to protect the health and safety of the worker whenever there is the slightest risk to either ? " Possibly, in theory, the State might beneficially interfere for both sexes, and in all cases.

2. As a matter of fact, however, there are some very grave objections to too much State action on the ground of health and safety. The object is to secure the health and safety of the worker. But it is obvious that, if he will be at the trouble to do so, a man can, as a rule, far better secure his own health and safety than any number of inspectors. The man who looks after himself and does not trust to others, has the best possible inspector always close at hand, and one always interested in and attentive to the matter he is inspecting.

3. The more, then, that the worker looks after his

own health and safety the better will his health and safety be protected. But it is an almost universal rule that, if a man sees another man appointed to do his business for him, he will neglect that business himself. It is the same in the human body. Put an artificial support round a muscle, and so do its work for it, and the muscle will soon become unable to perform its proper functions. So with men. If they rely on inspectors to look after them they will soon forget how to look after themselves.

4. But no one can look after one as well as one can look after one's self. Hence it is a mistake, except under special circumstances, to accustom grown men to depend not upon themselves, but upon inspectors. The true principle seems to be, that only in cases where the workers are, for some reason or other, incapable of properly looking after their own health and safety, should the State undertake the duty for them.

5. This is a large exception. Women and children, to begin with, cannot be expected to look after themselves efficiently. Clearly, then, they should when necessary have the help of the State; for even its inefficient protection is better than none. Again, in trades where to make proper provision for health and safety requires scientific and expert knowledge, as in the case of miners, the State can rightly interfere, for in these cases men cannot look after themselves. Again, there are many dangers, such as the dangers of bad drainage, which are beyond the control of the ordinary worker. In cases, then, where a man clearly cannot protect his health and safety it is reasonable that the State should interfere to protect him. We

should, however, try not to multiply these cases, but to limit them as strictly as possible. Our ideal should be not as much State interference as possible, but as little.

6. **Information as to the Condition of the Workers.**—There is one field in which State action in regard to labour can not only do good, but can do it without any risk of harm, and that is the collection and publication of information useful to the worker. Information on subjects connected with labour and the condition of the labourer is useful in a hundred ways. It is a light which enables the worker to see his way clear. For the worker who wants to make the best of himself, and to get the best return for his labour, it is essential to have sound and trustworthy information in regard to the general condition of the trade at which he works, and of the labour market generally.

7. If trade is bad and employment slack men know that it would be unreasonable for them to expect any large improvement in wages. When, however, trade is good and labour in high demand, they have a right to expect a change for the better. But before they take lower pay or ask for higher it is essential that they should know the true facts. Since the State can supply them with these without difficulty it is reasonable and right that it should do so.

8. **The Labour Department of the Board of Trade.**—In order that the workers shall be able to obtain accurate knowledge in regard to matters connected with labour an office has been established called " The Labour Department of the Board of Trade."

It is the business of this office to collect facts and figures of all kinds which may be useful to the workers, and to publish them in an easy and accessible shape. To show how wide is the scope of the Department we will give in an Appendix [1] the official Memorandum under which the Department was established.

9. **The Labour Gazette.**—Perhaps the most important and useful piece of work done by the Department is the issue of *The Labour Gazette*, alluded to above. It is published monthly, price 1d. There the workman, month by month, may find matter which will interest him in a hundred different ways—information as to strikes and arbitration, as to Co-operative Stores and Friendly Societies, as to the condition of the labour market, and as to various schemes for dealing with the unemployed.

1. *Beneficially.* Wisely; usefully.
8. *Scope.* The aggregate of things which the Department looks after.

Chapter XXVII

1. **The Government and Municipalities as Employers of Labour.**— Both the Central Government of the whole nation, and the Local Authorities, such as Municipalities, County and District Councils, and Boards of Guardians, come into direct contact with the workers as large employers of labour. For example, the Central Government employs

[1] See Appendix B, p. 223.

thousands of men in dockyards, arsenals, and factories, while the Town Councils, since they often own gas-works, water-works, and tramways, are constantly large employers of labour. What ought to be the duty of the Central Government and the Local Authorities in regard to the direct employment of labour?

2. The Government,—we use the word both as regards the Central and the Local Authorities,—when it employs labour, acts not like a private individual, but as a trustee either for the whole people or the locality. It is entrusted by them with the duty of doing certain things, and of doing them as efficiently and with as little burden as possible to the State or the locality. The first duty of the Government is, then, to see that the labour it employs is as efficient as possible, and procured in a manner as little burdensome as possible.

3. But this does not mean that the Government should pay the lowest possible wages, and work those in its employ the greatest possible number of hours. It has been shown that low wages and long hours do not produce cheap or efficient labour. It should, then, be part of the duty of the Government, as an employer, to pay wages sufficiently large, and to arrange the conditions of labour in other ways so as to attract the best class of labour.

4. It is specially worth while for the Government, central or local, to do this, because the Government cannot exercise the strict supervision which is exercised by the private employer. The Government cannot see half as easily as does the private employer that it gets full value for its money. But it is a matter of experience

that well-paid labour requires to be less closely looked after than cheap labour. Here, then, is another strong reason for the Government paying good wages when it acts as an employer. That will enable it to get the class of labour which works best under imperfect supervision.

5. But though, in order to get thoroughly efficient labour, the Government is justified in paying good wages and agreeing to short hours, it must be careful not to be an extravagant employer. To waste the public money by spending a larger sum on labour than is necessary to secure efficient work would be a breach of trust and disastrous to the public interests. For example, it would be a criminal waste of the resources of the nation if the Government were to pay £3 a week to dockyard labourers of a particular class for working six hours a day, when they could get the same men at £2 a week for eight hours a day.

6. No doubt it seems difficult to lay down in the abstract how the Government is to find out what wage will secure the maximum of efficiency, but in practice it is not really so difficult. If the Government pay the normal price for the best kind of labour, *i.e.* the price which private people will pay for the best class of labour, they are not likely to go far wrong. If, however, it should happen for any reason that in this class of labour the normal price is not enough to enable the labourer to keep himself in health and strength, then no doubt the Government would rightly pay him as much more as would enable him to maintain his health and strength. It *must* be bad policy for an employer to pay his men, even if they

will accept it, less than enough to keep them in health and strength, or to employ them for longer hours than are consistent with efficiency.

7. **The Government as a Model Employer.**—But though the Government would have no right to waste the money of the taxpayer or the ratepayer by paying the workers in its employ a wage higher than that which would secure the most efficient form of labour, it is quite right that the Government should act as a model employer—that is, that they should consult the happiness and convenience of the workers in every reasonable way, just as do the best private employers. They should, indeed, in all such matters as times and ways of paying, and arrangements as to meals and as to holidays, set an example to other employers.

1. *Arsenals.* Places where guns and weapons of war are manufactured.
5. *Criminal waste.* Waste so great that, to all intents and purposes, it becomes a crime.

Chapter XXVIII

1. **Duty of Workers whether with Hands or Brain.**—When we have spoken of workers we have not meant to confine our words to those who work with their hands. Those who are engaged in supervision and other forms of management are just as much workers as the weaver or miner. And just as it is of importance to the nation that the handicraftsman should do good work, so it is important that the

management of all forms of business and industry should be effective, honest, and intelligent.

2. A man has a choice between doing honest work, or scamp work, in book-keeping or in clerk's work, just as he has in carpentering or bricklaying. Indeed, the disasters which result from mismanagement and fraud in the conduct of a business are often more grievous than those which arise from bad hand-work. For example, the man who, through folly and idleness, or fraud, ruins a great bank, may bring misery on thousands, whereas the evils of a badly-joined door generally stop at injury to an individual.

3. **The Duty of the Community to the Workers.**—What duty has the community as a whole to the workers? Unquestionably it is the duty of the community to sympathise with, and to help on, every fair and reasonable effort of the workers to improve their material condition and to develop their intelligence. And for this plain and common-sense reason among others: If the workers of a nation are prosperous, intelligent, and hopeful, they will do far more and far better work than if their condition is depressed. If any one doubts that let him compare the work of a prosperous English cotton operative with that of a weaver in India or Japan. The Englishman, judged as a wealth and prosperity producer, is very much more capable than the Indian or the Japanese, and hence contributes very much more to the general welfare of the State to which he belongs.

4. It is then to the interest of the State—that is, of the community—that the workers should be well off in body and mind. A healthy, skilful, intelligent body of workers, upright and self-reliant in character, is

Photo. by H. T. Bool, Tottenham Court Road, W.C. THE POOL. (THE THAMES, NEAR LONDON BRIDGE)

a source of strength to the nation. An unhealthy, depressed, ignorant body of working men, without independence or the power of self-help, is a source of danger. That is why the community should sympathise with the workers in their efforts to secure better material conditions, or in other words, to make the best of themselves.

5. **The Good Citizen.**—One of the main objects of that association which we call a State is the making of good citizens; for if the greater part of the members of a State are not good citizens, that State is as inevitably doomed to ruin as is a rotten tree. How is the good citizen to be built up? First, by a faithful discharge of the homelier duties of life. Civic duty, the citizen's duty, begins in the life of the family, and expands with his occupations in trade, business, and profession. And especially can the duties of the good citizen be learnt, as we have shown, in the membership of self-governing societies. In helping to manage the affairs of a Trade Union, a Club, a Benefit Society, or a Co-operative Store, a man is learning how to help to manage and control the affairs of the State. Every one of these voluntary associations is a school of civic duty.

6. **Public Business the Concern of every Citizen.**—No citizen—that is, no member of the State—must ever allow himself to slip into thinking that the affairs of the State and its Government are nothing to him, and that he need not trouble about them. As well might a man say that the affairs of his own family are nothing to him. Patriotism—that is, love of one's country, and care and thought for her interests —is as necessary to national and social life as love of

wife and children, of father and mother, sisters and brothers, is to the life of the family. It was in no false or sentimental sense that the poet Wordsworth spoke of himself as feeling for his country as "a lover or a child."

7. That is how we should all think of our country. Just as we have duties to our family we have duties to our country, and duties which we can never shake off. We may sometimes think our country has acted wrongly, or has done us personally an injury, but that gives us no more right not to love our country than does an injury received from a father or mother gives us a right to hate father or mother. We may try, and ought to try, to make our country act rightly when we think it in the wrong, but no man can ever be right in not loving his country.

2. *Scamp work.* Badly done work made to look like good.

Chapter XXIX

1. **Just Legislation and Impartial Administration.**—Every man and woman naturally desires just legislation and impartial administration, that is, that only good and just laws should be made, and that when made they should be fairly carried out—carried out in such a way that no one class shall enjoy privileges beyond those of any other class. But it is no good merely to wish for this. People cannot expect good laws and just government unless they do their best to obtain those blessings. As well might one expect a good dinner and a com-

I

fortable bed, and make no effort to provide them. We shall never get good laws and just government unless all the citizens of the State realise that it is their first duty to pay attention to public affairs, and try their best to secure that they shall be well conducted.

2. **One out of Millions.** — It is no good for a man to say, "What is the use of my troubling, I am only one out of millions, and besides I am poor, and hold no important place in the world. What, then, can I do to secure good government?" To talk in that way is treason to the State. Though each one of us alone seems weak and of little account, the united efforts of a few thousand weak men can accomplish more than can the most powerful person in the State. In the Pacific Ocean there are islands which have been made to rise out of the sea by the work of the coral insects. These creatures by millions of tiny efforts have built up vast islands of hard rock.

3. So the efforts of millions of citizens build up a strong State. If the coral insects were one by one to say, "What is the use of building a cell so tiny that it is hardly visible?" there would be no island. In the same way, if the citizen says, "What is the use of my doing an invisible piece of work for the State?" there will be no State. In truth, each man by doing well that piece of public duty that devolves upon him—and some piece of public duty devolves on each one of us—may make the difference between a well and an ill-ordered State.

4. **The Citizen and the Vote.**—It is easy to see that if a man sits in Parliament, or on a Town Council,

or a School Board, or on the Committee of a Trade Union, a Club, or a Co-operative Store, he can help to produce good government by insisting upon justice and sound sense being the rule that governs all the transactions of these bodies. But take the lowest case—the case of a man who never has the opportunity to hold office, either in a public body or in a voluntary association. Even he can exercise a very great influence on public affairs. He has a vote, and that vote is the foundation of all laws and all Government —the cell of the coral insect.

5. Let him resolve that he will never give his vote for any man or any cause unless he is satisfied that he is giving it in the interests of right and justice, and let him persuade others to do the same, and he will be exercising an enormous influence on public affairs. When, too, he sees what he considers to be wrong and injustice being done in public affairs, let him resolve to set his face against it. However humble may be his circumstances, and however small may seem his power, his protest will in the end bring about a change. Injustice and wrong will not prevail for long if people steadily set their minds to get rid of them.

6. **The Citizen's Duty.** — "If we suffer injustice in connection with public affairs we have little right to complain, unless we have done our own duty." That is the principle which every good citizen should bear constantly in mind. When the good citizen hears of wrongdoing in public affairs he must not be content with mere complaints. He must ask himself, "Am I, myself, doing what I can to stop the wrong?" Till he can

truly answer "Yes," he is not doing his duty. When he can answer "Yes," he may feel assured that in the end the right will conquer the wrong.

7. Sometimes, no doubt, the right will be slow in coming, for error dies hard, but for all that he must not give up trying. He must bate nothing of heart and hope, but press right on, confident in victory. There never yet was a bad cause strong enough to stand against right and perseverance. These two forces are like Cromwell's Ironsides, of whom their leader said, "Truly they were never beaten." One without the other may be of no avail, but united they are invincible. The good citizen is he who does not weary in good doing, and the good citizen is what every man in the land should strive to be.

PART II

THE BRITISH EMPIRE

I.—THE EMPIRE

Chapter I

1. The Double Duty of a British Citizen.—In the case of many countries the inhabitants have only to consider their duties towards each other within the great association which we call the State. In the United Kingdom, however, the citizens have civic duties beyond those, which each inhabitant of the United Kingdom owes to the rest of the inhabitants of the United Kingdom. This comes from the fact that the United Kingdom is joined by political ties with certain English-speaking communities across the sea, and has, in addition, certain countries peopled by non-European races dependent upon it. In other words, the inhabitants of the United Kingdom, besides being British citizens, are citizens of the British Empire. But citizenship of the British Empire involves a whole series of complicated duties and responsibilities. Hence the Englishman must learn these in addition to those which belong to him in his simpler capacity of a citizen of the United Kingdom. Before, however, setting these forth it is necessary to describe the British Empire.

2. Perhaps the best general description of the

British Empire is that given by the great American orator Daniel Webster. He referred to the Empire "as a power to which Rome in the height of her glory was not to be compared—a power which has dotted over the whole surface of the globe with its possessions and military posts—whose morning drumbeat, following the sun, and keeping company with the hours, circles the earth daily with one continuous and unbroken strain of its martial airs." It is pleasant to think that this was written of our Empire by a man of the American branch of the English race.

3. **Great Britain and Ireland.**—The centre of the British Empire, the source from which that Empire was peopled or conquered, is the United Kingdom of Great Britain and Ireland — three kingdoms once separated, and containing Englishmen, Welshmen, Scotchmen, and Irishmen, but now united under one Queen and one Parliament. The way in which the United Kingdom is governed is described in a companion volume, and therefore need not be discussed here.

4. We will, however, note a verbal difficulty which sometimes arises in regard to the United Kingdom of Great Britain and Ireland. Many people find it awkward to use so long a title, and yet do not know how else to refer to our country without seeming to leave out of consideration the Scotch or the Irish. There should, however, be no difficulty in the matter. The word Britain covers not only England and Scotland, but Ireland also. When these islands first became known to the ancient world they were called the Islands of Britain—the bigger island which contains England and Scotland being called

THE S.S. "STIRLING CASTLE"

Great Britain, and the smaller island of Ireland, Lesser Britain. Hence to use Britain as including them both is perfectly correct. In the same way it is right to speak of the British Empire as meaning the Empire conquered by or settled from Britain.

5. Another difficulty that sometimes suggests itself is, "Is it fair to Scotchmen and Irishmen to talk of 'Englishmen' doing this or that, or of the rights and duties of Englishmen when we mean all the inhabitants of the United Kingdom, and not merely those belonging to the various counties of England?" We cannot help thinking that it is fair to do so; and for this reason. Except for a very few thousands, all the inhabitants of Britain speak English. Hence, when we speak of them as English or as Englishmen, we really use the word as a short form for English-speaking men. A man may be a Scotchman or an Irishman, and rightly proud of the race to which he belongs; but he is also an English speaker. To call him English, then, is merely to recognise the great fact that already binds us all together, and will continue to bind us still more strongly.

6. We say, and say with truth, that blood is stronger than water, and we may also say that the language which we learn from our parents, with which we win our wives, and in which we teach our children, is stronger than the claim of birth from a Saxon, a Jute, a Dane, a Kelt, or a Gael. Every one who speaks English as his mother-tongue has a right to be called English; and no one to whom the language of Shakespeare and Scott is native need feel ashamed to be called English. He is English, and why not call him what he is?

7. The Empire and its Divisions.—The great tracts of territory over which these little islands rule, or to which they are bound by ties of blood-relationship, must be divided into three divisions—(1) Those countries in which Englishmen, and by this we mean also Scotchmen and Irishmen and Welshmen, since, as we have said, they are all English speakers, have made a new England beyond the sea, countries which still continue joined to these islands, and acknowledge themselves as part of the British Empire; (2) Those countries which we have acquired by conquest, and in which dwell various races of men of dark skin and inferior civilisation; (3) Those countries which partake of the nature of both of these divisions, but belong to neither exclusively.

Chapter II

1. Greater Britain.—The first of these divisions has been well described by the phrase "Greater Britain." The old Greeks used to send out their citizens to build new cities and people new countries over the sea, and these new settlements, since they covered more ground than the old Greek cities, were called "Greater Greece." So in the same way the countries peopled from Britain may be called Greater Britain.

2. The first thing to note about the countries of Greater Britain is that they are self-governing, and that the bulk of the population, though they are outside Europe, is composed of people of European race, and usually of people of English race. These self-governing, English-speaking countries beyond

the sea, when spoken of separately, are generally called the Colonies — the word colony meaning, in modern times, a settlement of people who have left their old homes and established a new community in some savage land, but who remain connected with the mother-country, as the nation is called from which the settlers originally came.

3. The best way to explain what is the position of the self-governing colonies that make up Greater Britain is to take one of them as an example, and describe how it is governed, and what amount of influence is exercised on its affairs by the mother-country.

4. **New Zealand.**—The colony of New Zealand is a good example. It consists of two islands, together about the size of the British Islands, blessed with a temperate climate, and almost exactly on the opposite side of the world. To these islands, during the last eighty years, has flowed a more or less continuous stream of emigration from England, Scotland, and Ireland. At first the settlers were few, and neither numerous enough nor strong enough to defend themselves from the attacks of the natives,[1] or to organise a government without help from the mother-country. Accordingly, for the first twenty or thirty years the Government at home sent out officials to govern the colony.

5. Soon, however, the colonists grew strong enough to manage their own affairs, and they thereupon

---

[1] It should be said here that New Zealand, when first discovered, contained and still contains a certain number of dark-skinned natives called Maoris. These Maoris were not, however, civilised enough to make much use of the country in which they lived, nor were their numbers sufficient to make them occupy any large portion of it. They did not cultivate a thousandth part of the soil.

demanded the right of governing themselves — a demand which they were perfectly justified in making, since, though capable citizens of English race, they were not able to send representatives to the Parliament at Westminster, and to help to make the laws there.

A MAORI

Their demand was granted, and Parliamentary Government was established in New Zealand very much on the model of our Government at home. The constitution of New Zealand resembles that of all the communities of Greater Britain. First, there is a

Governor, who acts in regard to the affairs of New Zealand much as the Queen acts at home—that is, though he is nominally the head of the State, and names the ministers who carry on the Government, he only names those in whom the country and Parliament have confidence.

6. Next comes the Parliament, which consists of a Lower House chosen by the whole body of the electors, like our House of Commons, and of an Upper House, whose members are nominated by the Governor,[1] and who sit for seven years, and act much as does our House of Lords. The Parliament may levy any taxes and, practically, may make any laws it pleases as far as the affairs of New Zealand are concerned, and thus the colony is properly described as a self-governing community. Just as in England the Queen's assent is required to the laws, so in New Zealand the Governor's assent in the name of the Queen is necessary.

7. Theoretically, the Parliament at Westminster has power also to make laws in regard to New Zealand, but in reality this power is never used. The Imperial Government, i.e. the Government here in England, has also the power to require the Governor not to assent to —that is, to veto—laws which they think injurious. Originally this power was often exercised, but now it is tending to die out, and would never be used in regard to laws which only affected New Zealand. The only case in which a Governor would withhold his assent from an Act passed by a self-governing colony, would be the case of an Act which would in some way or other interfere injuriously with the rights of the mother-

---

[1] In a good many of the colonies the Upper House is elected, but by a rather different set of electors, voting in different areas.

Photo. Valentine and Sons, Dundee.

FOREIGN AND COLONIAL OFFICE

country, of other colonies, or of friendly foreign nations, or in some other way do harm to the British Empire as a whole. Finally, though the self-governing colonies appoint their own judges, suitors may, in important cases, and where the law is not clear, appeal to the Judicial Committee of the Privy Council, a Court of Appeal which sits in London.

8. **Colonial Independence.**—Perhaps it may be said, that since the mother-country has so small a right of interference in the case of the self-governing colonies they must be considered independent, and that the slight connection with them maintained by the appointment of the Governor and the right of appeal in important law cases is hardly worth preserving. That, however, is a very mistaken view. Our present union with the colonies of Greater Britain is one which is well worth preserving, both from their point of view and from ours; while it is maintained, and there is no reason why it should not be maintained for ever, it prevents the English-speaking inhabitants of Greater Britain becoming "foreigners," either as regards each other or as regards themselves and the mother-country.

9. **The Bad Results that would follow Colonial Independence.**—Think for a moment what would be the situation created if the various colonies became independent states, in no sort of union with the United Kingdom of Great Britain and Ireland. In that case, when an Australian came either to England, or to Canada, or to South Africa, he would be in law a foreigner, and unable to claim the full rights of citizenship. The Englishman would be in the same position when he went over sea. Now it is different.

Since we all acknowledge the same Queen and the same flag, and are all citizens of the same Empire, the Australian, or the Canadian, or the South African can travel to any part of Britain, or of Greater Britain, and find himself everywhere a full citizen. The inhabitant of Britain can do the same.

Chapter III

1. **The Value of the Common Citizenship.**—Not less is the common citizenship useful to the inhabitants of the Empire when they are in foreign countries. Let us take an example. Tasmania is a small and therefore a weak country. If, then, Tasmania was independent, and a Tasmanian were badly treated in some foreign country, it is quite possible that the Tasmanian Government would be unable to get any redress. The Foreign Power would say, We cannot give you redress, knowing full well that Tasmania could not enforce its claim.

2. But as long as the connection between England and Tasmania is maintained, every Tasmanian is also a British citizen, and therefore the whole force of the Empire would be exerted to enforce the just claims of any injured Tasmanian. As long as we maintain a common citizenship with the lands that make up Greater Britain, we are maintaining something which is most useful and valuable—something which helps to prevent war and enmity, and to give the English-speaking race a far better chance of development than it could obtain without that common citizenship.

3. **The Future of our Race.**—Everything points to the English-speaking race becoming the dominant one in the earth,—spreading over all the lands and seas, and teaching other peoples its language and its laws. But if this dominance is to last and be for good it is essential that our race should recognise its kinship and its common origin. If it does not, the ages that are to come may but repeat those that are past. That is, we may see the world divided between a number of independent states growing year by year more hostile and forgetful that they are of the same blood. If, on the other hand, the common citizenship is maintained, we may see the reign of peace gradually spread over half the world, and the British Empire may in time teach the other nations how to avoid war and national hatreds.

4. **Advantages to England of maintaining the Union with the Colonies.**—It is sometimes said that it is easy enough to show that the self-governing colonies gain from the connection with the mother-country, but far less easy to show that the mother-country gains from her connection with them. Our fleets, it is argued, protect the colonies from the risks of war, and our ambassadors and consuls, all the world over, see that no citizen of the Empire is injured by the action of foreign powers. That is a clear gain to the colonists, but since we at home pay for the fleets and ambassadors and consuls the gain to us is much less clear. No doubt, put like this, Greater Britain may be made to appear a burden rather than a support. Those who argue thus are, however, very shortsighted. The colonies may need protection now. In fifty years' time they may be able to

give it. Before children of five or six are sixty it is probable, indeed we may almost say certain, that there will be more English-speaking people living in Greater Britain than there are now in these islands. But if the colonies have not become foreign countries, but are still united to us by a common citizenship, they will doubtless stand by us in any trouble or peril.

5. How the Colonies may Help the Mother-land. —When a father spends money on his children, and does what he can to help them, he may at the moment seem to be getting nothing by his expenditure. When, however, those children have, owing to his care, thriven in the world, and are able to repay his devotion, who can say that he did unwisely to stand by them and help them when they were weak and young? So with the mother-country and the colonies. But though self-interest alone would teach us to stand by the colonies and protect them, we must not act merely out of self-interest. Though honesty is the best policy, a man who is only honest for that reason is not an honest man.

6. So the mother-country, if she merely stood by the daughter states because she looked forward to being helped by them in years to come, would not be acting a mother's part. We must protect the colonies of Greater Britain, and make their cause and their best interests ours, not because it will pay us to do so, but because they are our own flesh and blood, men of the same race and tongue, and ruled by the sense of right and duty. We must cleave to them because, to use Milton's words, they are "God's Englishmen" over sea, and we are "God's Englishmen" at home.

7. Imperial Federation. — Many people both in

Britain and Greater Britain believe that some day it may be possible to draw still closer the ties that unite the self-governing colonies, and to create what is called an Imperial Federation—that is, a Parliament and a Government for the whole Empire. Whether that will ever come about, or whether it will not be better to leave things as they are, and to rely upon the common citizenship and an alliance for defence and security is, however, a matter which cannot be profitably discussed for many years. Possibly in fifty years many things will have become easy which now seem difficult, and Imperial Federation will be no longer a dream. Meantime, we can all agree upon maintaining the common citizenship and the feeling of unity which at present exists. That gives us all that is absolutely necessary, and until we are sure of something better, let us all join hands to maintain it. As long as we feel that we are citizens of one Empire, whether we live in Britain, in Australia, in New Zealand, in Canada, or at the Cape of Good Hope, and can never become foreigners to each other, we have secured the future of the British race.

1. *Redress.* Reparation for a wrong done.
3. *Dominant.* Ruling.
4. *Shortsighted.* *I.e.* they do not look ahead, to try to see what may happen in the future.

Chapter IV

1. Imperial Co-operation. — Even if we cannot manage to create an Imperial Federation, and resolve for the present to make a common citizenship the

Photo. F. G. O. Stuart, Southampton.
OFFICER, VICTORIA MOUNTED RIFLES.

essential bond of the British Empire, there are many useful things which we may do by co-operation between the different communities of the Empire.

2. **Imperial Defence.**—For example, there is no reason why, each according to its strength and size, the various colonies should not contribute towards the expenses incurred for defending the Empire. No doubt for a long time the chief burden must fall upon the United Kingdom, but little by little the young English states beyond sea will be able to do their share. Already Australia contributes towards the fleet which guards her coasts, and within the next thirty or forty years we may expect to see a great development in this direction. The time is probably not far distant when the representatives of an Australian commonwealth will meet not only the statesmen of the mother-land, but the representatives of the Dominion of Canada and of a united South Africa, to determine on what share each shall take in the defence of the Empire.

3. **The Forces that Prevent the Break-up of the Empire and tend towards Co-operation for Defence.** —When the colonies are asked to help keep the Empire together, they will be sure to see the advantages of union against disintegration. The forces that work for keeping the Empire together, and for maintaining a system of close political alliance and of common citizenship between its different parts, are much stronger than those which tell for separation.

4. Let us notice what are the forces that tell against the colonies becoming independent powers and assuming the position of foreign states. First, there is the feeling of race and brotherhood,—one of the noblest,

perhaps the noblest feeling that a human being is capable of experiencing. Though he may be shy of expressing it in words, what speaker of the English tongue, sprung from English-speaking parents, does not in his heart feel proud and glad that he is "one of God's Englishmen," that, in Carlyle's words, he is "a subject of King Shakespeare," and that he belongs to the united people, English, Scotch, and Irish, who can boast of Cromwell and Knox, Blake and Nelson, Marlborough and Wellington, Burke and Canning, Pitt and Fox? But the man who thanks God he is of the race, which is first in liberty and laws, as in arms and letters, is sure to feel that the brotherhood of those who speak the English language must be maintained, and that the lands peopled by the English kin must not be allowed to drift apart and become weak and isolated states.

5. Next, the practical sound sense of Englishmen is against breaking up the Empire. Men of business notice that commercial affairs go better between countries which are united than between those which stand to each other in the relation of foreign states. Whatever the reason, trade goes easier when conducted under one flag than under two. Why, then, do away with something that smooths the road of commerce? Next, the self-governing colonies feel that as long as they remain part of the Empire they have a claim to share in the immense possessions which the United Kingdom holds in Asia, in tropical Africa, in South America, and in the West Indies.

6. Though people as yet hardly realise the fact, Australia feels a very deep interest in India, for Australia (the word means East Asia) understands

that she is an Asian state. But this being so Australia does not want to lose her right to share in our possession of India, Ceylon, and the Straits Settlements. Instead, she wishes to assert her interest in India, for she knows that as her population increases and her trade grows that interest increases. In the same way, Canada does not want to lose her interest either in the West Indies, in British Guiana and British Honduras, or in Hong-Kong and the Malay Peninsula.

7. Cape Colony, again, does not want to lose her interest in Uganda and British East Africa, or in our territory on the Niger. Lastly, Australia, Canada, and South Africa do not want to lose touch with each other. But, practically, they can only keep hold of each other by keeping hold on Britain. Lastly, the colonies feel that they have many enemies, that many hungry glances are cast at their fair lands, and that united they are far less liable to attack than when standing alone. Thus sentiment, self-interest, the desire to share in the glorious heritage of Britain in her subject lands, and lastly, the sense of self-preservation, all work in favour of maintaining the connection between Britain and the self-governing colonies. Imperial defence, then, is a matter in which the mother-country and her daughter states can and ought to co-operate.

8. **Imperial Penny Postage.**—Another matter in which co-operation could and ought to take place is the establishment of an Imperial Penny Post. Nothing unites people more effectually than cheap and quick means of communication. For this reason it is proposed that a penny stamp should carry a letter to

and from any place under the Union Jack. If people by spending only a penny can communicate with each other, it matters comparatively little whether they are seven or thirty days' journey apart. If once a penny Imperial post were established, and were maintained for ten years, we should hear very little more of breaking up the British Empire. Millions and millions of tiny threads spun between households in Canada, and Australia, and South Africa, and England, and Scotland, and Ireland, would have created a cable that no force would have the strength to sever. Imperial Penny Postage is a matter which we should all work for.

9. **Other Forms of Co-operation.** — In various other ways we may co-operate with the colonies. For example, it would be well if from time to time the colonies and the United Kingdom considered the subject of laws affecting the whole Empire, and endeavoured to bring those laws into harmony. For instance, it would be a good thing that the commercial laws of the whole Empire should be the same, and also the laws affecting shipping; and as far as possible the criminal law and the marriage law. No wise man would care to see any attempt made to force the laws on these matters into harmony, but wherever co-operation for producing uniformity of laws could be secured, the effect would be good.

10. **Imperial Coinage.** — Yet another form of Imperial co-operation might be found in the adoption of one coinage for the whole Empire. At present we have the dollar in Canada, the rupee in India, and the sovereign in Australasia, South Africa, and the United Kingdom. Why should we not agree to adopt

a common coinage? If we did, perhaps the best to adopt would be the dollar—the coin of our kinsmen in America. It has the advantage of being used already by nearly seventy millions of English-speaking people; and it would have the further advantage of giving us a decimal coinage.

    3. *Disintegration.* The breaking away of parts.
    4. *Letters.* Literature and learning, forming a whole.

II.—THE SELF-GOVERNING COLONIES

Chapter V

Canada and Newfoundland

1. Canada.—We have said something about the general aspects of the self-governing colonies; we will now deal with them more in detail, taking in order the three great self-governing groups of British North America or Canada, Australia, and South Africa. The Canadian Dominion embraces all that part of the North American continent which lies to the north of the United States, except Alaska, which belongs to the United States. It is inhabited by about 5,000,000 people. Though the climate is cold the soil of the southern parts of Canada is very fruitful, and the land contains vast stores of minerals.

2. The fact that Canada stretches from the Atlantic to the Pacific Ocean, that it has splendid ports and harbours on both oceans, and that on the Atlantic side a mighty river, the St. Lawrence, gives access to the heart of the country, makes the geographic position of Canada a very favourable one. No country in the world has such splendid water-communication as Canada. Its lakes, rivers, and canals

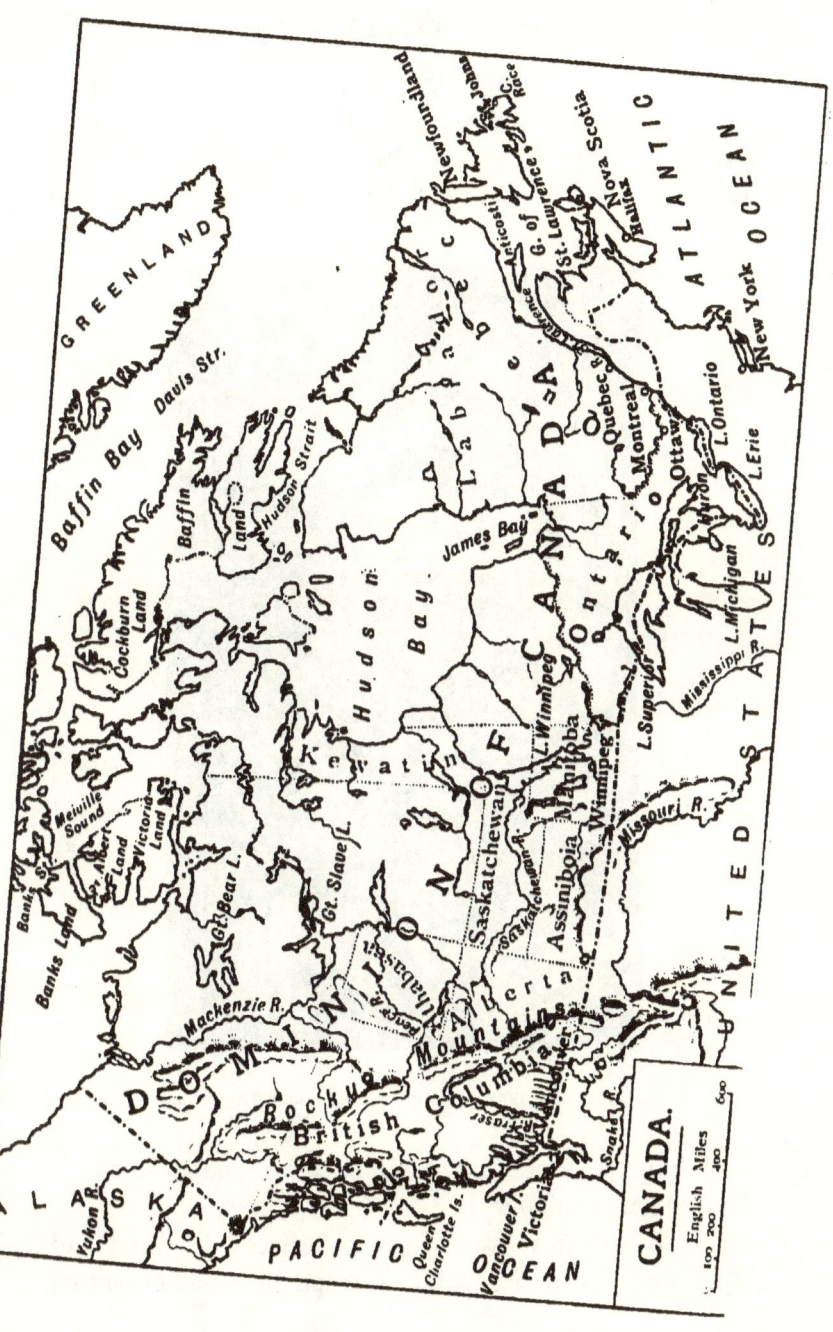

give ship-transport throughout the Dominion. Lastly, there stretches from ocean to ocean a line of railway called the Canadian Pacific Railway, by which travellers can be conveyed with great rapidity, as well

From a Photograph

AHT INDIAN WOMAN OF THE COAST OF BRITISH COLUMBIA

as with great ease and comfort from the western to the eastern hemisphere.

3. The quickest way of going between England and Japan and Northern China is to go by steamer across

From a Photograph by Topley.

the Atlantic to Halifax, from Halifax by train to Vancouver on the Pacific coast of Canada, and from Vancouver in a steamer to Japan or China. The Canadian Pacific route is also as quick as any other for reaching many parts of India, and Australia, and New Zealand.

4. **The Government of the Dominion.** — The Government of the Canadian Dominion is what is called a Federal Government—that is, the Canadian Dominion is made up of the provinces of Ontario, Quebec, Nova Scotia, Cape Breton Island, New Brunswick, Manitoba, the Western Territories, Prince Edward Island, and British Columbia. Each of these provinces has a separate government for managing its local affairs, consisting of a Lieutenant-Governor and a Parliament. The whole Dominion is, however, united in a single central government which governs all the more important affairs of the Dominion.

5. This central government, which is seated at Ottawa (3540 miles from London), is made up of a Governor-General, and a Parliament consisting of a House of Commons chosen by the people, and a Senate of eighty members chosen for life by the Governor-General. There are so many senators for each province, and when a vacancy occurs the Ministry of the day advise the Governor-General whom to appoint. There is also a Privy Council, from whom the Ministers, as in England, are chosen by Parliament to advise the Governor-General.

6. **The French in Canada.**—Before we leave the subject of Canada we must note one important fact. Canada is not peopled entirely by people of English race, or by speakers of the English language. The province

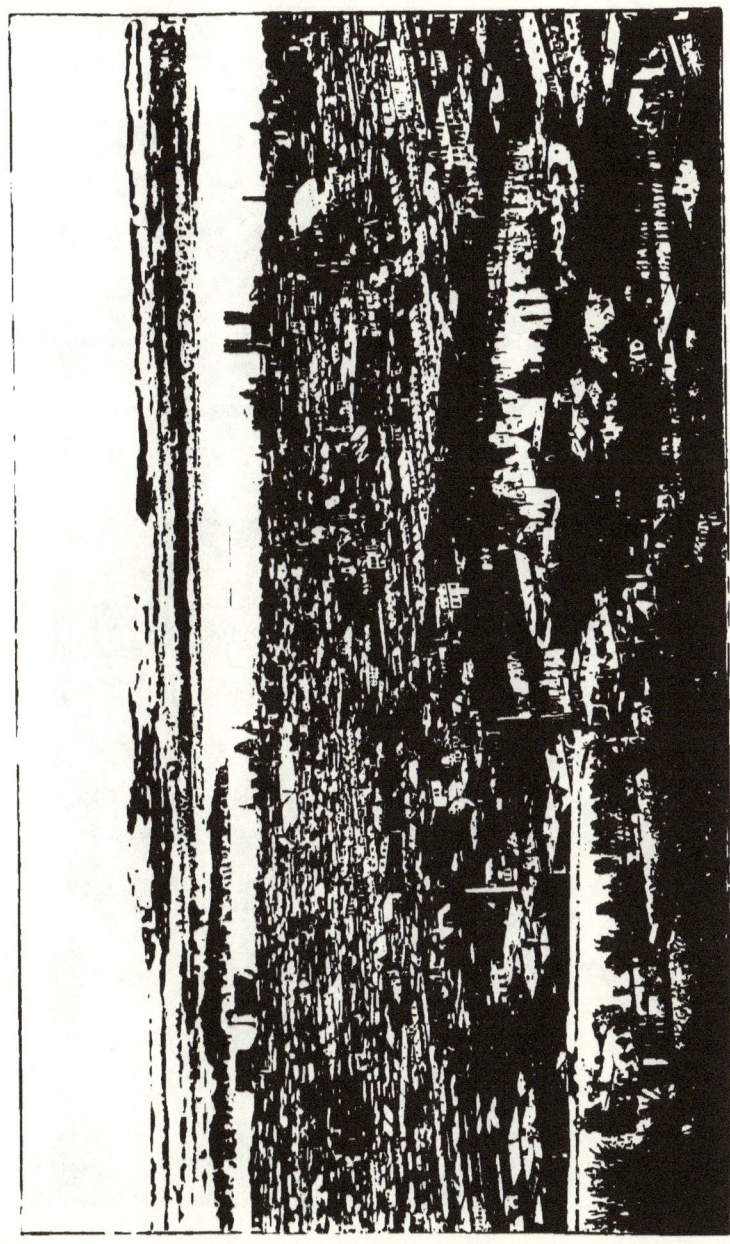

From a Photograph by Topley. PARLIAMENTARY BUILDINGS, OTTAWA, WITH RAFTS OF TIMBER ON THE RIVER.

of Quebec was conquered by us from the French, who had originally colonised it, and its inhabitants still speak French and are Roman Catholics by religion. They are, however, absolutely loyal to the Dominion and to England, and are quite willing to remain a part of the British Empire. Till recently the Canadian inhabitants of French origin have numbered nearly half the total population, but the latest returns show that the English-speaking population is now in a considerable majority.

7. **Newfoundland.** — Newfoundland is a very large island (the twelfth largest in the world) off the coast of Canada. Some day it will, no doubt, join the Dominion as a province. At present it is an independent, self-governing colony, with a Governor and a Parliament, consisting of a Legislative Council of not more than fifteen members, appointed for life, and a House of Assembly elected by the people. The population is nearly 200,000. Newfoundland possesses on the mainland of America a portion of the coast of Labrador. The chief industry of the colony is the cod-fishery in summer, and the seal-fishery in winter. The inhabitants are, in fact, either fishermen or farmers. The climate is healthy, but wet and often foggy.

Chapter VI

Australia

1. **Australia.** — The next great self-governing division of the British Empire is Australia. Australia

AUSTRALIA AND NEW ZEALAND

CHAP. VI   THE SELF-GOVERNING COLONIES   119

is the island continent on the opposite side of the globe to England and south-east of India. Australia

QUEENSLAND WOMEN

is divided into five colonies — New South Wales, Victoria, South Australia, Queensland, Western

Australia, and to these must be added the island of Tasmania, which lies near the coast of Australia, and which is sure to join the Australian colonies when they definitely agree to establish the great commonwealth of which they have already formed the plan.

2. **The Australian Commonwealth.** — Sooner or later the whole of Australia will be federated into

MELANESIANS

a dominion somewhat after the model of Canada. Already the colonies have met and drawn up a constitution, and have agreed to call their federation, when it is made, the Commonwealth of Australia, —a good old English name, and implying what should be the foundation of every state—and we may expect that before very long arrangements will be made for

COLLINS STREET, MELBOURNE.

carrying out the excellent scheme of government upon which they have agreed. We shall, therefore, not describe Australia colony by colony, but as a whole.

3. **The Geography of Australia.** — Australia is the largest island in the world, and is about as big as Europe. At present its population is between three and four millions. Of these the majority are white people of English blood. There are about 200,000 natives, but they are apparently incapable of civilisation and are rapidly dying out. The climate of Australia is very various, but almost everywhere healthy. The north is tropical, but even there the country is habitable for Europeans, while in the south the dry, invigorating air has proved well suited to the full development of the English race. The soil is naturally fruitful, and capable of producing in abundance all that man requires. The only drawback is the tendency to drought. When, however, this is counteracted by irrigation, it is not too much to say that there is no land in the world capable of producing more than Australia.

4. There are two physical features of Australia which ought to be remembered. Though the continent is so large there are no great rivers, no great lakes, and no great mountains. No river which is navigable for any distance inland can be named; and the highest mountain, Mount Townsend, is only 7256 feet above the sea. Australia has a large amount of mineral wealth. Coal is extensively worked, and gold and silver have been and still are found in large quantities.

5. **The Government of Australia.**—The governments of the Australian colonies, with a few minor differences, conform to the model which we have

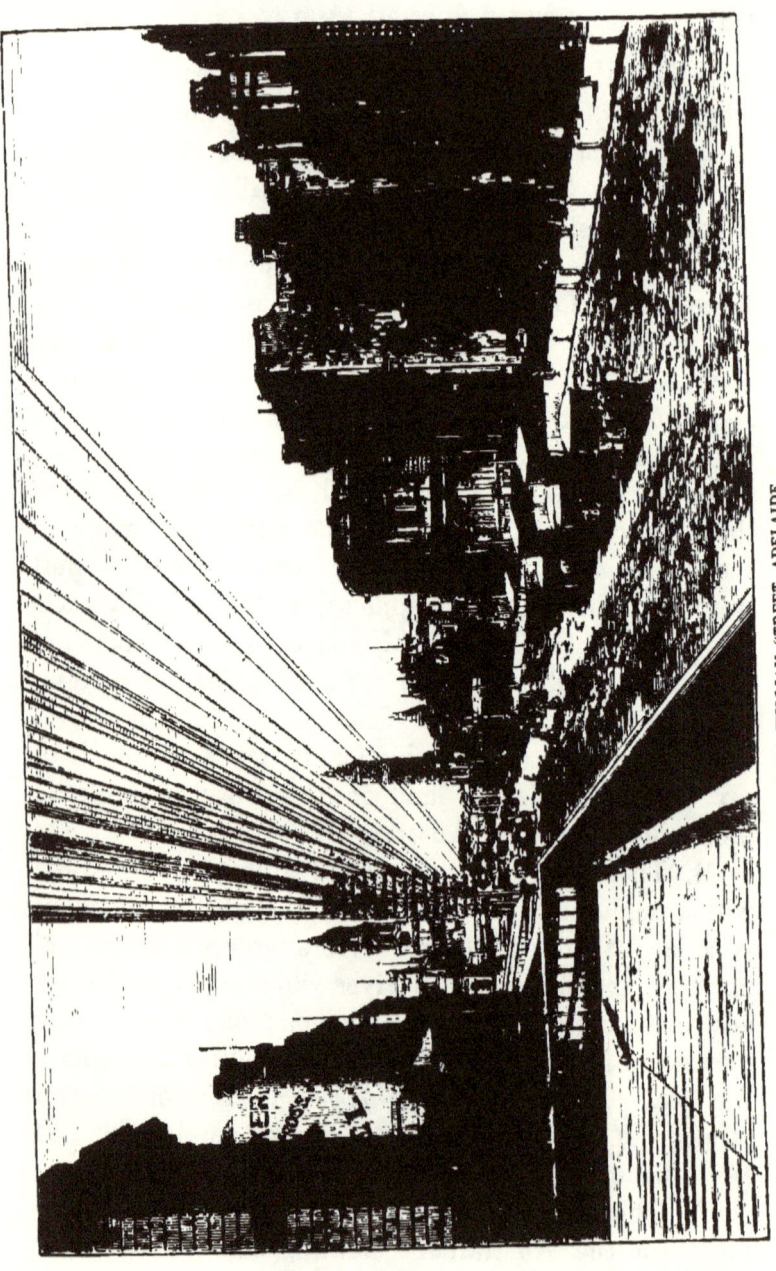

KING WILLIAM STREET, ADELAIDE

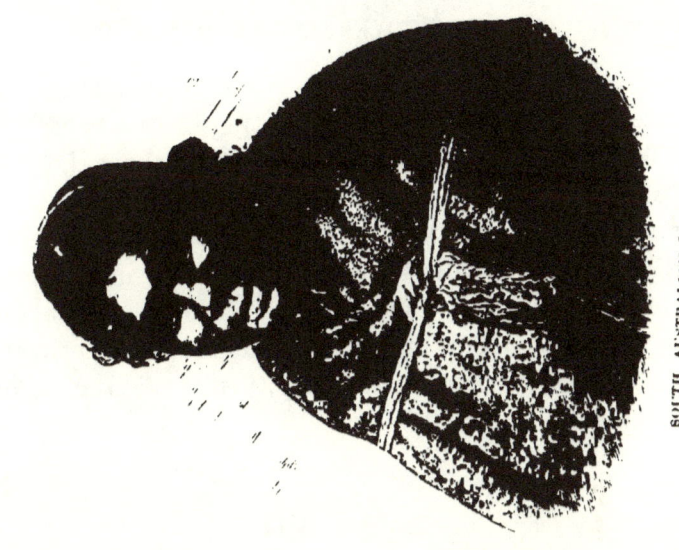

SOUTH AUSTRALIAN (WOMAN)

SOUTH AUSTRALIAN (MAN)

already given. There is in each a Governor, a Ministry, and a Parliament consisting of two houses.

6. **Tasmania.**—Tasmania is an island about the size of Ireland. It is temperate in climate, fertile, full of forest producing the most valuable woods, and containing minerals of all sorts. The native inhabitants have entirely died out, and the white population now numbers about 155,000. The Government consists of a Governor, a Ministry, and two Houses of Parliament.

Chapter VII

South Africa.

1. **South Africa.** — We now come to the last of the three great groups of self-governing communities. South Africa, like Australia, is made up of three or four colonies, but before long it, too, is destined to become federated. Whether it will adopt the name of Dominion or Commonwealth or United States we cannot say, but it is practically certain that we shall some day see a united South Africa.

2. The colonies that make up South Africa are, (1) Cape Colony, (2) the colony of Natal, both self-governing colonies; (3) British Bechuanaland, a Crown colony; (4) the Bechuanaland Protectorate; (5) the possessions of the Imperial South Africa Company; and (6) the Boer Republics, named the Orange Free State and the Transvaal. These must each be described separately, so various are the arrangements under which they are governed.

3. **Cape Colony.**—Cape Colony is a self-governing

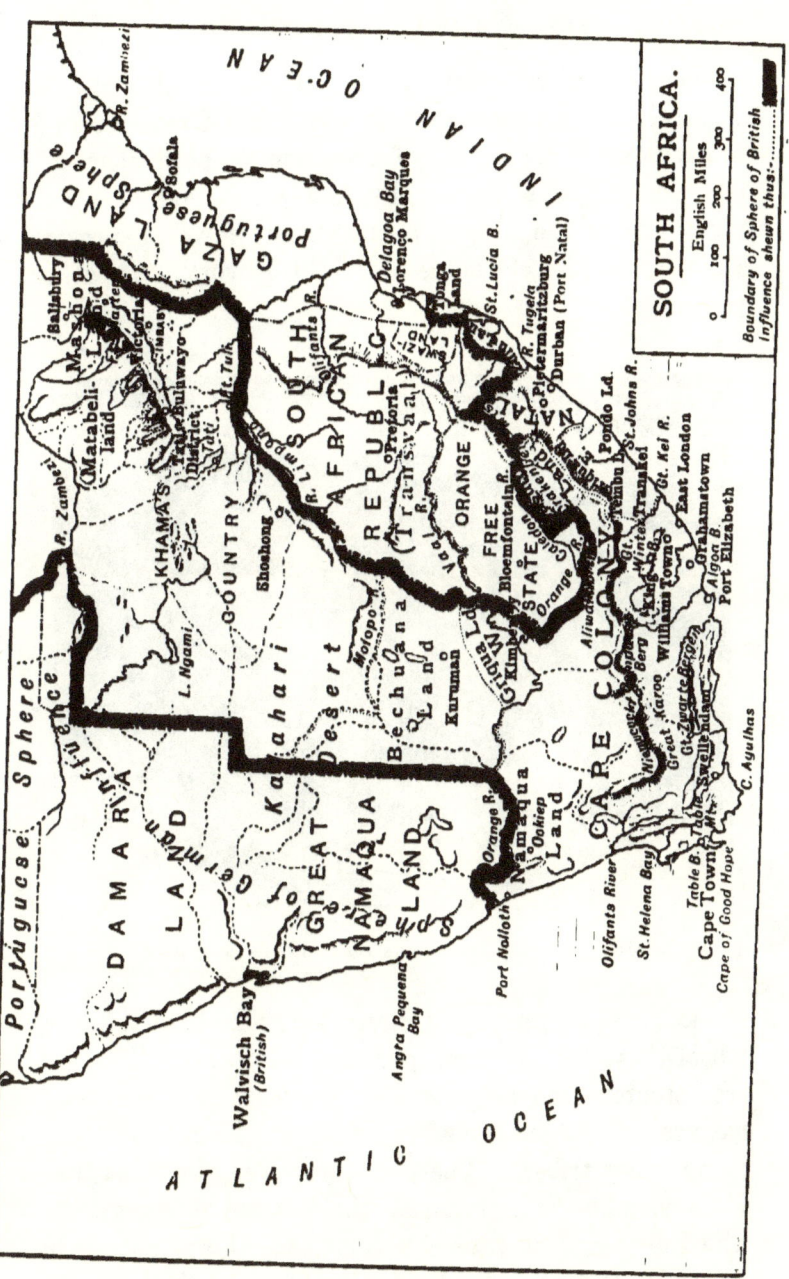

colony, organised very much on the model of the Australian colonies—that is, there is a Governor and a Parliament, consisting of two houses, both of which are elected, and elected by the same voters. The members of the Upper House must, however, possess £2000 worth of land, or £4000 worth of other property.

TABLE MOUNTAIN AND DEVIL'S PEAK, CAPE OF GOOD HOPE

4. There are in Cape Colony 1,527,224 inhabitants, but of these only a fourth part are Europeans. The rest are coloured men of various kinds, most of them being natives of Africa—Kaffirs, Fingoes, Hottentots, and many other tribes. There are, however, about 14,000 Malays, who have entered the colony as emigrants. The Europeans, it must be remembered, are not, as in Australia and New Zealand, all people of English race

and English speech. About half or more are of Dutch, or German, or French origin, and speak Dutch, for the colony was originally occupied by the Dutch, and till about a hundred years ago belonged to Holland. It is for this reason that the laws used in the Cape Colony, in a great many particulars, resemble those of Holland. The climate of the Cape is healthy, but warm, and the soil, where there is water, very fertile. The interior is mountainous.

5. **Natal.**—Natal is another self-governing colony on the usual model, at present entirely independent of the Cape, and situated on the east coast of South Africa. Its total population is about half a million, but of these only some 57,000 are Europeans. These Europeans are, however, almost entirely people of English origin. The climate is hotter than that of the Cape, but healthy, especially in the mountain districts inland.

6. **British Bechuanaland.**—British Bechuanaland is what is called a Crown colony, the meaning of which term is explained later. It is situated to the north of Cape Colony, and is as yet very little developed. There are only 60,000 inhabitants in all, and of these not more than about 5000 are Europeans. The climate is not a very healthy one owing to its extreme dryness, and to the great differences between the night and day temperatures.

7. **The Bechuanaland Protectorate.**—The Bechuanaland Protectorate is a large tract of country situated to the north of British Bechuanaland. It has as yet been very little explored, and there are at present not more than 500 Europeans living in it.

8. **The Possessions of the British South Africa**

Company.—Beyond British Bechuanaland and the Bechuanaland Protectorate lie the possessions of the South Africa Company. This territory belongs to England, but was handed over to a company under certain conditions. The company, as long as it lasts, governs the territory and levies the taxes, and acts, as it were, as the agent of the Home Government. Not very much is yet known about the company's territory, except that there is gold in it, and that some of the land is very good farming land. A part of the territory was at one time occupied by a fierce tribe called the Matabele, but in 1893 the company made war on the Matabele and destroyed their military organisation.

9. **The Boer Republics.**—Within British South Africa, and yet not strictly belonging to the British Empire, are two republics called the Orange Free State and the Transvaal or South African Republic. These republics were founded by the Boers or Dutch settlers from Cape Colony. Their inhabitants are a set of hardy, God-fearing farmers, and though they have sometimes quarrelled with the English, no Englishman should desire to treat them with anything but respect. Though, as far as their internal affairs are concerned, the two republics are independent, they acknowledge the supremacy of the United Kingdom. This supremacy is, however, hardly more than nominal, and is only exercised to prevent the republics making agreements with foreign countries which are dangerous to the interests of England.

10. **Future of South Africa.**—Though it is probable that Australia will follow the example of Canada sooner than South Africa, it may be confidently pre-

dicted that before very long we shall see the whole of South Africa, including even the Boer republics, formed into a commonwealth under the British flag — a commonwealth in which the old prejudices and jealousies will be forgotten, and in which Englishmen and Dutchmen will join in making a state as powerful and prosperous as the Canadian Dominion.

III.—CROWN COLONIES

Chapter VIII

1. **Crown Colonies.**— The next division of the British Empire which we must consider are the Crown Colonies. These are possessions which are for the most part peopled by non-European races of dark colour, and governed, not by persons elected by themselves, but by a Governor and other officials sent out from England. The reason for this difference is a very simple one. Those colonies which are peopled by men of English and European race can provide themselves with a better Government than we could provide them with from here. Hence they have been given responsible Government.

2. Those colonies in which the English or European element is very small can be best governed, it is found, by the Crown Colony system. The native dark-skinned populations are not fit to govern themselves —they are too ignorant and too uncivilised—and if the government is left entirely in the hands of the small number of whites who may happen to live in the colony, they are apt not to take enough care for the interests of the coloured inhabitants. The simplest form of Crown Colony is that to be found in some of

the smaller groups of islands in the West Indies. Here a Governor is sent out from England, and he—helped by a secretary, a judge, and other officials—governs the island, reporting his actions to the Colonial Office, and consulting the able officials there before he takes any important steps.

3. In most cases, however, the Governor has a Council of some kind to assist him. This Council is either nominated from among the principal persons in the colony, or else is elected by the inhabitants. In some cases—Jamaica or Barbadoes, for example—the Council has very great power, and the type of Government may be said to approach that of the self-governing colonies.

4. It would be impossible to describe all the Crown Colonies separately. We will therefore take the several groups into which they naturally fall, and say something as to each group.

The American Group of Crown Colonies.

5. **The American Crown Colonies.**—The following is a list of our American Crown Colonies:—

(1) The Bermudas (a collection of small islands), population 15,700.

(2) The Bahamas (a collection of small islands), population about 50,000.

(3) The island of Jamaica and its dependent islands, population 600,000.

(4) The Leeward Islands (a collection of small islands), population about 126,000.

(5) The island of Barbadoes, population 180,000.

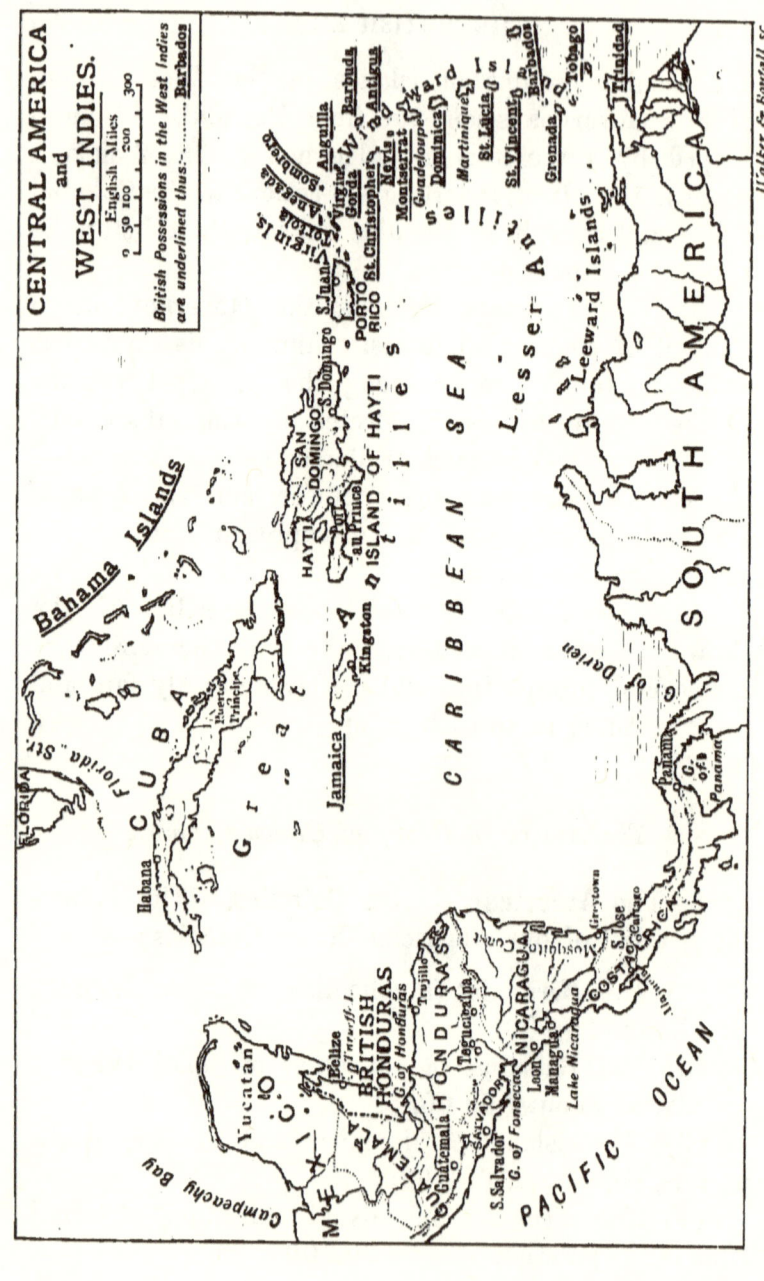

(6) The Windward Islands (a collection of small islands), population about 148,000.

(7) The islands of Trinidad and Tobago, population 210,000.

(8) British Honduras (a settlement on the coast of Central America), population 32,000.

(9) British Guiana (a settlement on the coast of South America), population 282,000.

PORT ROYAL, JAMAICA

6. **Characteristics of the American Group.**—All these colonies have much the same features. They are nearly all situated within the Tropics, and have therefore climates too hot for European settlement on any large scale, or to allow Europeans to do work in the open air. They are, also, all inhabited by the descendants of the negro slaves brought to them before England had realised the wickedness of

the slave-trade, and had made the negroes free. Again, almost all of them are interested in the production of sugar. Under these circumstances, it is clear that it would be greatly to the advantage of all the colonies concerned if they were to be joined under one confederation. Jamaica is nearly in the centre of the group and would probably make the best capital. The various colonies could keep their present forms of internal government under Lieutenant-Governors, but the whole confederation could be ruled by a Governor-General.

The Falkland Islands.

7. **The Falkland Islands.**—The Falkland Islands are a group of islands forming a Crown Colony, and lying south of Cape Horn, that is, off the extreme end of the continent of South America. There are only some 1890 inhabitants in all. The climate is rainy, but not unhealthy. Owing to the damp, grain will not ripen; but there is excellent pasturage for sheep, which thrive well in the Falklands.

The Pacific Group of Crown Colonies.

8. **The Fiji Islands.** — Besides the great self-governing colonies of the Pacific—Australia, Tasmania, and New Zealand—there are in the Pacific several Crown Colonies. The most important of these are the Fiji Islands. They have a population of 121,000, but only 3000 of these are Europeans. Scattered throughout the Pacific, in what is called Polynesia, are

many other islands which belong to the British Empire, but none of these are large enough or important enough to be worth considering separately.

Chapter IX

The African Crown Colonies.

1. Crown Colonies in West Africa. — The African Crown Colonies are numerous. We have already mentioned one in South Africa, British Bechuanaland, and will now give the remainder, which are situated on the West Coast of Africa. They are—

(1) Sierra Leone, population 74,000, only 200 of whom are whites.

(2) Gambia, population 14,000, very few of whom are whites.

(3) The Gold Coast.

(4) Lagos, population 100,000, very few of whom are whites.

The climate of all these West African colonies is unhealthy, and Europeans find it very difficult to live in them.

The Mauritius Group.

2. **The Mauritius Group.** — In the Indian Ocean, *i.e.* between Africa and India, are the Island of Mauritius, the Seychelles Islands, and the Island of Rodrigues. Mauritius, which was originally conquered from France, is an important island. Its inhabitants number about 370,000, of whom some are "coolies"

or labourers from India, some Negroes, some Malays, and some Chinese. The whites, who are not very numerous, are either English or else descendants of the original French settlers. These still talk French. The Seychelles Islands have a population of about 17,000, of whom very few are whites. Rodrigues has a population of under 2000.

Our Mediterranean Colonies.

3. **Our Mediteranean Colonies.** — In the Mediterranean England holds three possessions: Malta,

VALETTA, MALTA

Gibraltar, and Cyprus. These may all three be counted as islands, for Gibraltar is only joined to the mainland by a narrow strip of sand, and could be turned into an actual island by digging a canal not a quarter of a mile long.

4. **Malta.**—Malta, situated in the middle of the Mediterranean, is a flourishing and populous island held by England for military and naval purposes. It has nearly 166,000 inhabitants. The Maltese are a race apart, and speak a language which is partly Italian and partly Arabic. Though the Government is that of a Crown Colony, the people elect a Council, which is allowed to have a large share in the govern-

GIBRALTAR

ment of the island. Malta is the station of our Mediterranean fleet. We keep there besides a large force of soldiers.

5. **Gibraltar.**—Gibraltar is a huge mass of rock close to the mainland of Spain, and situated at the entrance to the Mediteranean, which at this point is only some seven miles broad. On "the Rock," as it is called, is a small town of Spanish-speaking people. We, as a rule, keep at Gibraltar a force of about 5000 soldiers.

6. **Cyprus.**—Cyprus, an island off the coast of Asia Minor, is not strictly speaking a part of the British Empire, but remains nominally part of the possessions of Turkey. Since, however, it is garrisoned by English soldiers and governed by English officers it differs very little from a British possession.

Eastern Crown Colonies.

7. **Ceylon.**—The great dependency of India must be treated separately, but there are a number of Crown Colonies in the eastern hemisphere which must be enumerated here. Chief among these is Ceylon, the great island which lies at the point of the Indian Peninsula. Ceylon, though nominally a Crown Colony and under the control of the Colonial Office, is governed more after the fashion of an Indian province than an ordinary Crown Colony. The people of Ceylon number about 3,000,000, and the Government consists of a Governor, an Executive Council, and a Legislative Council of eighteen members chosen by the Governor, among whom are representatives of the various native races inhabiting the island. The climate of Ceylon is hot and the soil fertile.

8. **Aden.**—Aden is a fortified port on the Arabian coast at the lower end of the Red Sea. It is of great importance as a coaling station, though not as a colony.

9. **The Straits Settlements.**—Half-way between India and China are the Straits Settlements, a series of British Crown Colonies on the west coast of the Malay Peninsula, and commanding the Straits of Malacca. The population—the bulk of which con-

sists of Chinese and Malays — numbers 512,342. Singapore, the capital, is a large town, and one of the greatest ports in the whole world—a circumstance probably not unconnected with the fact that Singapore is a free port, and that no Customs duties are levied on any ship entering its harbour. The Government is like that of other Crown Colonies. Singapore is almost on the equator, and hence the climate hardly varies, but is the same throughout the year. Considering this fact it is not unhealthy.

10. **Hong-Kong.**—Hong-Kong is a small island off the coast of China. Its population is 221,441, of whom the greater number are Chinese. The commerce of the port is very great. The Government is conducted by a Governor and a Council of six members, and a Legislative Council of eleven members.

IV.—PROTECTORATES

Chapter X

1. **Protectorates.** — Protectorates are possessions of the British Empire situated in more or less savage countries, in which a regular administration has not yet been established. When a piece of territory has been proclaimed a British Protectorate no other nation has any right to annex or occupy it, and the native population would be protected by the British Government from any aggression either on the part of foreigners or English people. A Protectorate is usually governed by a Commissioner or Administrator sent out from England, who has under him other English officers.

2. Very often the power and authority of the native chiefs is not superseded, but the Commissioner governs through them and in their names, giving them his advice and help in the management of their affairs. Our Protectorates are chiefly situated in Africa, but there is one in New Guinea. Certain of the islands of the Pacific are also under our protection.

African Protectorates.

3. **British East Africa.**—In East Africa a British Protectorate extends over the island of Zanzibar, the

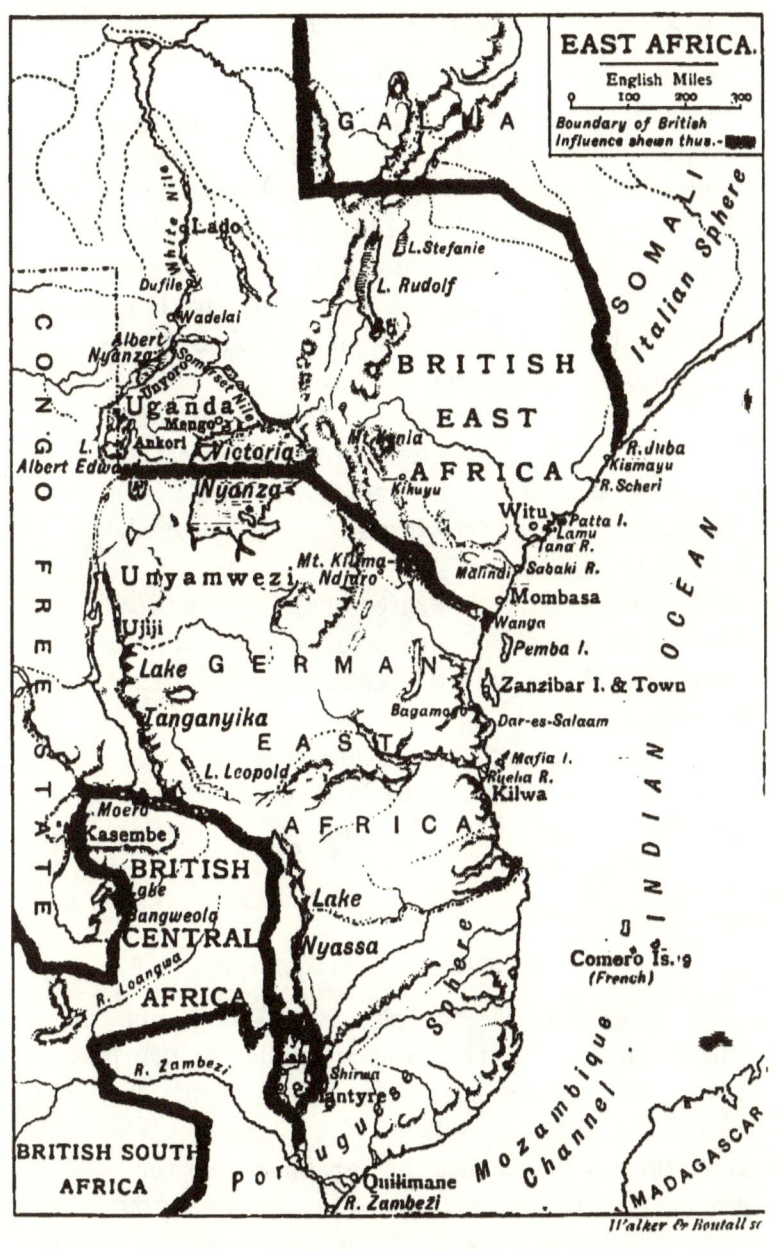

coast on both sides of the settlement of Mombasa, and a large portion of the interior country. The country on the coast is very unhealthy and quite unfitted for the residence of Europeans, but inland the climate changes, and the country called Uganda, situated on and near the shores of the great lake called Victoria Nyanza, is well suited to Europeans. The country is governed by an English Commissioner and European assistants.

4. **Nyassaland or British Central African Protectorate.**—This Protectorate lies in the central part of Africa, and on and around the great Lake Nyassa. At present the Protectorate is administered by a British Commissioner.

5. **Bechuanaland Protectorate.**—The Bechuanaland Protectorate has been mentioned in our account of South Africa, and will doubtless some day be included in a United South Africa.

6. **Niger Coast Protectorate.**—The Niger Protectorate is situated on the West Coast of Africa, and includes a portion of the coast of Africa near the mouth of the Niger.

Western Pacific Protectorate.

7. **Western Pacific Islands.**—A large number of islands in the Pacific Ocean are under British protection. British influence and British rights in these islands are maintained by a High Commissioner. His chief duty is to see that the inhabitants of the islands are not injured or kidnapped by British subjects or other Europeans. The High Commissioner is generally the same person as the Governor of the Fiji Islands.

8. **New Guinea.**—In the Pacific Ocean there is another Protectorate—that of New Guinea. New Guinea is a large tropical island north of Australia. The north part of the island belongs to the Germans, but the south, which is near the coast of the Australian colony of Queensland, is part of the British Empire.

Chartered Companies.

9. **Chartered Companies.**—Certain portions of the British Empire have been handed over to and are governed by what are called Chartered Companies. These companies were primarily formed for the purposes of trade, but Parliament has given them the right to govern and make laws for the uncivilised countries in which they carry on their trading operations. In the charters under which these companies act it is provided what they may do and on what subjects they may make laws, and also that if they do not govern well the charters will be forfeited. There are in all four chartered companies —three in Africa and one in Asia.

10. **South Africa Company.**—The South Africa Company holds a vast tract of territory to the north of Cape Colony. As yet this territory has been very little explored, but in most parts the climate is good, and gold is found in many districts.

11. **British East Africa Company.**—The British East Africa Company holds that portion of the coast of East Africa which is opposite Zanzibar. In all probability, however, the British East Africa will soon cease to exist as a governing company, its powers

being taken over by arrangement with the British Government.

12. **Niger Company.**—The Niger Company's territory is on the West Coast of Africa, and includes the mouth of the great river Niger, and a portion of the course of that river. The Niger valley is quite unfit for the prolonged residence of Europeans, but many valuable products are found in its forests, and the company has a large trade.

13. **North Borneo Company.**—In the great island of Borneo, in south-eastern Asia, a tract of territory has been handed over to the North Borneo Company, a company which, like those in Africa, combines the work of government and trading.

14. **Other Possessions.**—We have enumerated most of the important possessions of the British Empire, but a certain number of small islands and other insignificant possessions have been left out of account; these are to be found in the Roll-Call of the British Empire [1] given later.

14. *The Roll-Call of the Empire.* See Appendix C, p. 226.

V.—INDIA.

Chapter XI

1. **India and its Government.** — We have left to the last, in order that it may stand by itself, and apart, the great dependency of India. This is by far the greatest of those possessions of the British Islands which are directly controlled by a minister responsible to Parliament, and so by the votes of English citizens. Questions connected with India must therefore be studied carefully by every man who wishes to exercise well and usefully the political power which he possesses, by means of the vote.

2. **The Importance of India.** — The fate of the United Kingdom and of India have come to be bound together so closely that it would now be well-nigh impossible to destroy one without destroying the other. If India were to be ruined England would almost infallibly be destroyed also. Hence every Englishman has the strongest possible motive for understanding about India, and for seeing that she is properly governed, that is, governed in a way which will make that huge collection of countries prosperous and happy. Canada, Australia, and South Africa can look after

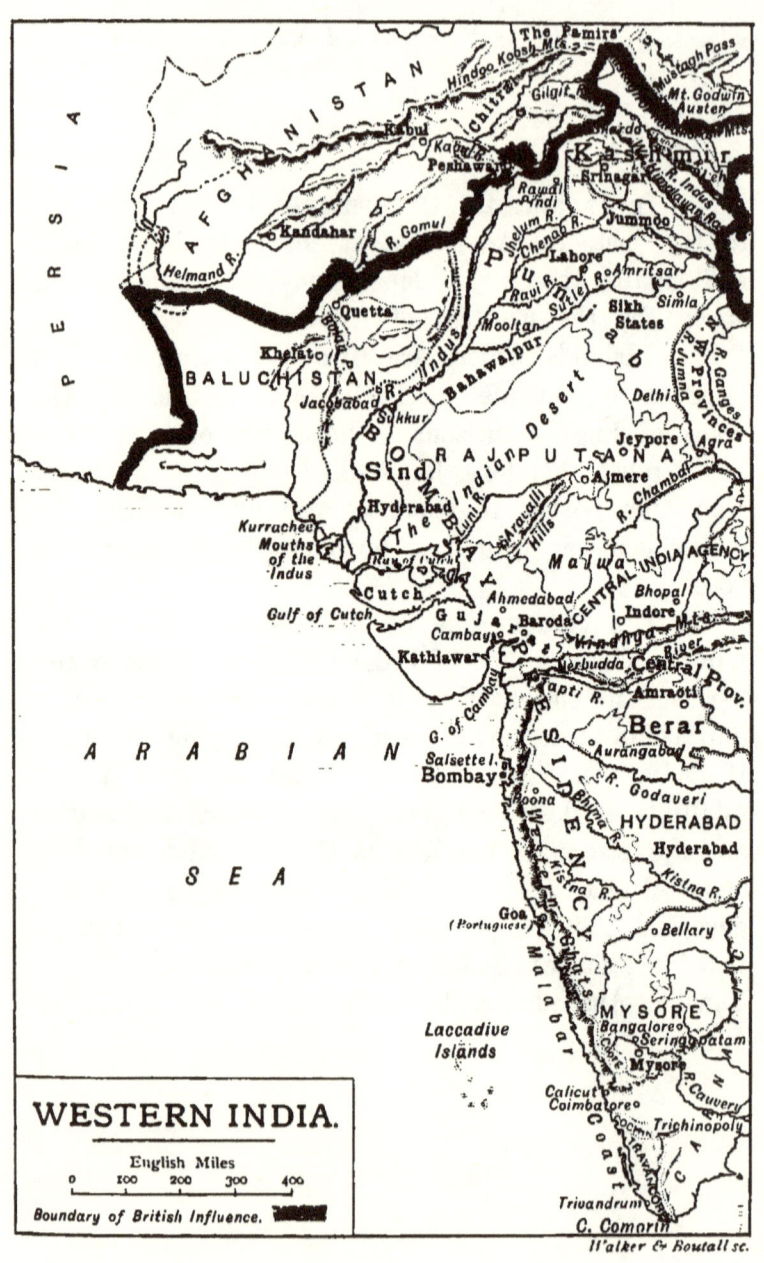

themselves better than we can look after them, and all we need do in their case is to maintain a brotherly feeling towards the Englishmen and others who inhabit them, and to work with them for the common good.

3. In the same way many of the Crown Colonies and Protectorates can almost be left to themselves, and need comparatively little attention. As long as we send out good men to govern them they are not likely to get into danger. The government of India is, however, a task so great, and the responsibilities and risks connected with it are so immense that no Englishman can afford not to consider them.

4. **What India is.**—India is a vast peninsula which, roughly speaking, is surrounded on two sides by the sea, and on one side by a great circle of lofty mountains. It is thus very much cut off from the rest of the world, and only easily approached by sea. India is in size about as large as Europe without Russia, and is, therefore, to be considered as a continent rather than a country. India contains nearly 290 millions of people, and every ten years some thirty millions more, or nearly as much as the total population of the United Kingdom, are added to the population. In other words, England has every year in India alone a population of 3,000,000 added to the Empire. India is in size thirteen times greater than the United Kingdom, and has some eight times the population.

5. **The Chief Thing to Remember about India.** —The chief thing to remember about India is the fact that it is a continent and not a country. It is an entire mistake to think of India as if it were a place like England, France, or Germany, only bigger, and

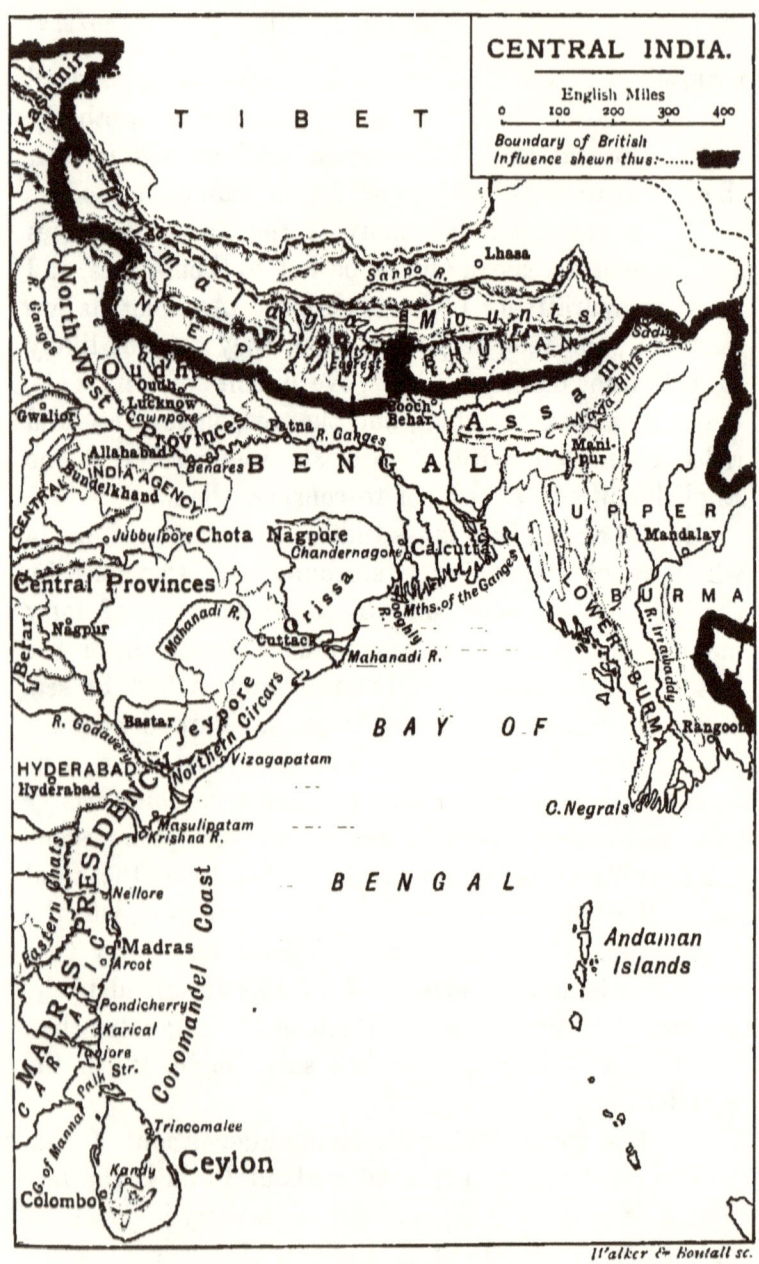

inhabited by a single people, speaking the same language, having the same, or very nearly the same religion, thinking the same thoughts, pursuing the same aims, regarding each other as men of the same kin, and feeling to their native land the same love, affection, and devotion that Englishmen feel towards England.

MÁRÁTHÁ PANDITS (BRAHMANS)

6. India is, instead, a collection of a vast number of peoples, races, and states, differing widely from each other in race, in language, in religion, in ways of life, and bound to each other by no common feeling. If you were to ask a native of India whether he felt any love towards India as his fatherland, he would stare at you in astonishment. He might feel for his own race, his

own state, or his own religious sect, but to expect him to feel a patriotic feeling towards India would be like expecting a Frenchman to regard the continent of Europe with a sense of love and veneration.

7. **The Word India.** — The word India is not even known to most of the inhabitants of India. If

RÁJPUTS

you take an Indian from the south of India and put him down in the north or the east, he will not only be unable to speak the language of the people, but will very likely find himself a stranger to many of the religious observances and customs going on around him. In fact, he will feel himself and will be almost as much a stranger as an Englishman suddenly landed in India. We must remember, then, to be very careful how we use such phrases as "the people of India ask for this," or "the people of India require that." When we hear them being used we should ask,

BURMESE GENTLEMAN AND LADY

"Which of the many peoples of India do you mean," for the words by themselves have no meaning.

8. **Religion.**—The people who inhabit the great continent which we call India have five main religions: Hinduism or Brahminism, Mohammedanism, Buddh-

ism, the religion of the Sikhs, and Christianity. There are, besides, a good many different forms of Paganism, but these need not be named separately. Of the five chief religions the Hindus number about 190 millions,

PATHÁNS

the Mohammedans about 54 millions, the Buddhists about 7 millions, the Sikhs about 2 millions, and the Christians about 2 millions. Other religions number about 7 or 8 millions. The Buddhists chiefly live in Burmah, to the east of India, and the Sikhs in the north-west. The rest of India is occupied in common by the other religions we have named, the Mohammedans being strongest in the north.

9. As a rule the mass of the ordinary Indian popula-

TODAS, ABORIGINALS OF THE NILGIRI HILLS

tion professes Hinduism, but scattered among them are many millions of Mohammedans and a smaller number of native Christians. But though the votaries of these religions have lived side by side for so long the feeling between them is by no means good, and but for the interference of the British Government they would be perpetually at war with each other. The Hindus are forbidden by their creed to kill cows or to eat beef, and regard it as a profanation to have a cow killed in their neighbourhood. The Mohammedans, on the other hand, not only eat beef, but often sacrifice

DRAVIDIAN HILL-MAN (AFTER FRYER)

bulls as part of their religious ceremonies. Hence the Hindus and Mohammedans are always quarrelling over the question of cow-killing, and riots often occur which can only be put down by the action of the English soldiers.

10. At the same time both Hindus and Mohammedans despise and hate the native Christians, and look

with unfriendly eyes on the Jews, the Parsees, and, in fact, all those who differ from them in faith. There is, except among the educated, little or no feeling of toleration, and the peace is only kept between the various religions by the strong hand of the British, who insist that persecution must cease. No doubt there are many good and enlightened natives of India who hate persecution as much as Englishmen do, but they are unfortunately a very small minority. The mass of the people think themselves quite justified in hating and despising those who differ from them in religion.

9. *Profanation.* A grave insult to all religious ideas.

Chapter XII

1. **Races.**—The different races of India do not correspond to the religions. Originally, no doubt, the greater part of India was occupied by a Hindu race professing the Brahminical religion. Many hundred years ago, however, great bands of Mohammedan conquerors entered India from the north-west and settled in large numbers. But not all the Mohammedans in India are descended from these invaders. The Mohammedans converted, generally by force, a great many of the Hindus, and thus many of the Mohammedans really belong to the same race as the Hindus.

2. **Language.**—The languages talked in India are as numerous as those talked in Europe, and quite as different the one from the other. The chief are Bengalee, Hindustanee, Tamil, Telegu, Burmese, but there many others besides these.

Photo. F. Frith and Co., Reigate.

GOVERNMENT HOUSE, CALCUTTA

3. **The Government of India.**—The task of governing this vast continent and all its various races and religions has fallen to the people of the United Kingdom. How it came about that we conquered India cannot be told here, but it may be said that the conquest was the result of the desire of the English race to trade and of their inability to tolerate misgovernment. We went as traders, but finding that the misgovernment and confusion which prevailed in India prevented our trading, and that we could easily put the country into better order, we gradually began to take over the management of the country. Thus, little by little, we assumed possession of the whole of India. It thus happens that every Englishman has become responsible for the government of India.

4. **A Double Trust.**—The government of India, it must never be forgotten, constitutes a double trust. It is a trust to govern India at one and the same time in the true interests of the people of India, and in the true interests of the English people. It must not be supposed, however, that there is or can be any conflict between these two sides of the trust. As long as we consider the true interests of the people of India we shall do no injury to the interests of our own country. As a matter of fact, the interests of both are so closely bound up that we cannot separate them.

5. **The Ruin of India means the Ruin of England.**—This can be easily explained. If we were to grow careless and negligent in the work of government in India, and were to allow the different races and religions in India to fight with and persecute each other, the whole continent would soon be in as great a state of anarchy, misery, and confusion as it was

when we came to India. This would be terrible for the people of India. It would be quite as terrible for the people of the United Kingdom. And for this reason. If anarchy broke out in India we should have to do one of two things—either to reconquer India or to abandon it. But to reconquer India after having let it get into a state of anarchy would cost thousands of English lives and millions of money, which would have to be paid by the taxpayers of England, and would fall as a grievous burden on them.

6. Not less would be the burden if we left India. The result of that would be that the immense trade which we now do with India would fall off and perish, and that the large sums of money which we have lent to India to build railways, to dig canals and reservoirs, and to perform a great many other useful works, would be entirely lost. No interest would be paid on the loans, and the capital would be destroyed. The effect of this would be felt by every man, woman, and child in England. Hundreds of thousands of men who now get their living by the trade with India would be left without work or hope, and at the same time the large number of people who live upon the interest paid by railways and other Indian loans would no longer be able to give employment to English labour.

7. Depend upon it, the ruin of India must mean the ruin of England. It is, then, for our own sakes, as well as for the sake of the Indian people, of the utmost importance that we should govern India wisely and well, and in such a way as to secure peace and prosperity.

8. **The Selfish View.**—Some people think that it

would have been better for England if we had never gone to India, and never taken the great responsibility which we have undoubtedly taken. This, however, is a somewhat selfish way of looking at the matter, for no one can doubt that we have very greatly benefited the inhabitants of India by undertaking their government. Read the accounts of what was the state of India a hundred and fifty years ago, that is, before we held any large part of India, and you will realise what a noble work England has done in India.

9. **India as it was.**—This is what an Asiatic, not a European, and therefore, a man not prejudiced by European ideas, said of the state of India before we conquered it: "No man," said a Persian traveller of the eighteenth century, "of his own choice will ever live in India: without compulsion he will never consent to a long residence there . . . unless he be one who unexpectedly arrives at wealth and distinction, or from lack of moral strength . . . becomes tranquil there, and habituates himself to the life." Another native writer, speaking of the state of India before our coming, says much the same: "Villainy was practised in all its forms; law and religion were trodden under foot; the bonds of private friendship and connection, as well as of society and government, were broken; every individual, as if in a forest of wild beasts, could rely upon nothing but the strength of his own arm." A hundred such quotations might be given to show the misery of India as it was.

Chapter XIII

1. **India as it is.**—India as it is presents a very different picture. Here is a description of India at the present day given by a modern historian:[1]—

"When we look at the India of to-day, north and south alike, we find a difficulty in believing that it is peopled by the near descendants of the beings thus described [*i.e.* by the native writers just quoted]. The population is dense, almost too much so, but it is free from crime, and orderly to an unusual degree. Roads, canals, railways, and busy manufacturing and commercial communities are everywhere to be seen. Five universities and nearly one hundred thousand public schools provide all grades of instruction; a large revenue is raised with a very low rate of incidence. The country has passed, in a few generations, from anarchy to the reign of law."

2. **Our Present Duty.**—It is, however, hardly worth while to consider whether we did right in going to India. We are there, and our duty now is to consider how to do our best and not to worry ourselves with scruples about the past. A man who is firmly fixed in a trade is a fool if, instead of trying to do his best in it, he is always wondering whether he should not do better in something else.

3. **How can India best be governed by England?**—It might be supposed that the answer to this question was "By letting the Indians govern themselves." We see that in the United Kingdom the best form of government is obtained by letting the people

[1] *History of India*, by G. H. Keene.

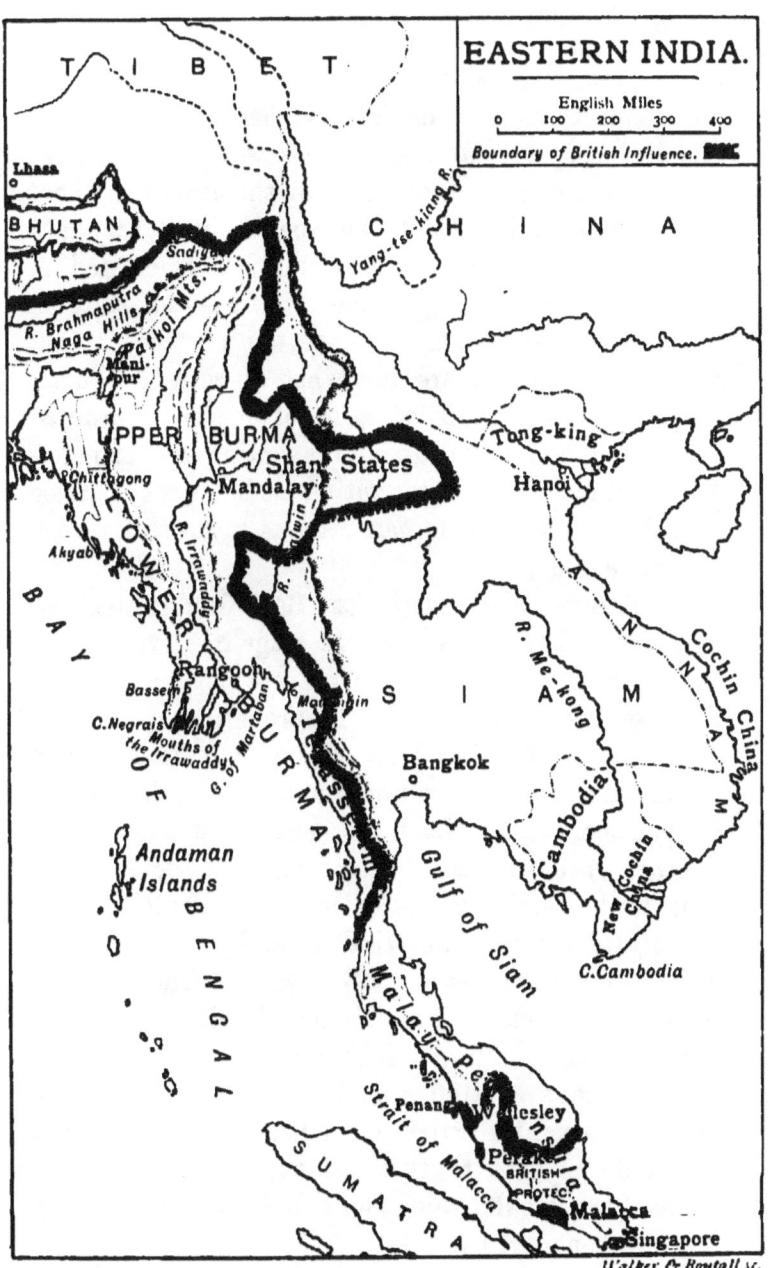

govern themselves, and it appears natural at first sight to consider that what holds good here will hold good in India. As a matter of fact, however, if we tried to let the people of India govern themselves without English help and control, we should in a very few years bring back the state of things which existed in India before the coming of the English—the state of things described above. The reason of this is that the people of India are not what is called a homogeneous nation, that is, a nation of one or of kindred races using one language and adopting the same or similar religious creeds, tolerating each other's customs and beliefs, and agreeing generally as to how they wish to be governed.

4. **Things Necessary for Self-Government.**—Nations that have arrived at the stage of development which renders them homogeneous are not only fit for self-government, but can only be properly governed in that way. India, however, is not a nation, but a seething mass of contending races, creeds, languages, and political ideas. Each race and creed differs from the other races and creeds as to how the government ought to be carried on, or as to what should be the ideal of the state. The Hindus think it as terrible a crime to kill a cow as to kill a man. The Mohammedans eat beef. The Hindus think that India belongs to them. The Mohammedans, on the other hand, despise the Hindus, and profess to think that they are the rightful rulers of India. "If the English would only go back to their island," say the Mohammedans, "we would rule India by the sword with which we conquered it."

5. **Differences among the Hindus.**—But even

the Hindus do not agree among themselves. The fierce Mahrattas, who used to levy *chout*, or blackmail, throughout India, and pillage and rob at their heart's content, hold that they have a natural right to lord it over the mild, timid, and peace-loving inhabitants of Bengal. The Rajputs, again, declare that but for the English they would spread their rule over a great part of India ; while the Sikhs are not less sure that they were meant by Providence to overrun the whole peninsula. Lastly, the fierce hill tribes who live in the great girdle of mountains that surrounds India look down from their crags at the rich plains, and consider that they suffer a grievous wrong from the English in being deprived of so rich a piece of plunder.

6. **The Result of a Native Domination.** — Remember that if any one of these races or creeds was to conquer, its idea would not be to rule the conquered land to the best advantage, and to make it flourish even more than before its conquests. That is what a European conqueror does, but not what an Asiatic. Take, as an example, the efforts of the Austrians in Bosnia and Herzegovina, the provinces annexed by them from Turkey. They have done everything possible to make the Provinces flourish, from making railways to building schools and hotels. The Asiatic notion of conquest is very different. The Asiatic believes that the conqueror has a right to live upon the conquered, and to treat them as his slaves.

7. Remember that the moral feeling of the Asiatic is quite different to ours in regard to slavery. He does not consider it as necessarily a crime to enslave a human being, and this fact tinges all his notions of

political domination. Any one can see from these facts that it would be quite impossible for us to leave India to govern itself, granted that our object was to get for India the best government possible under the circumstances. Leaving India to govern itself would mean giving the word for a fierce struggle for supremacy among the various races and creeds of India.

8. **Governing India through its Natives.**—But, it may be said, even if we cannot leave India to govern itself, why should we not govern India through its natives? At present India is in the last resort governed by a number of Englishmen, who direct the whole administration, and fill all the highest posts, whether as judges, collectors of revenue, engineers on public works, or officers of the native army. Why, it is said, should not Indians be gradually substituted for these Englishmen, and India be governed by Indians—the English army being, however, kept to keep watch that the peace was not broken, and to enforce tolerance among the different creeds and races?

9. **The Objection to this Course.**—The objection to this proposal is one which is absolutely fatal. You cannot altogether substitute Indian natives for Englishmen if you are to keep hold of your ideal of giving India the best government possible, because Indian natives would not govern India nearly as well as Englishmen. The reason why this is so, is again to be found in the fact that India is not a homogeneous country.

1. *Anarchy.* The condition of being without government of any kind. Greek, *an-*, negative prefix; *archos*, a ruler.
3. *Homogeneous.* From the Greek, *Homogenēs*, of the same race.

Chapter XIV

1. **Confidence in the Governors essential to Good Government.**—It is a most important thing that the governed should have confidence in the fairness of their governors.

2. But if you are to take an Indian district as a whole, and to consider whether a native or an Englishman will inspire most confidence in its inhabitants, you will find that it is the Englishman. Almost every Indian district is peopled by both Mohammedans and Hindus, and some have several other religious creeds in them, besides being inhabited by people of more than one race. But this being so, if you give supreme power to a Mohammedan, it seems unfair to the Hindus, if to a Hindu, it seems unfair to the Mohammedans. Nor is this the whole difficulty. The man fitted to take charge of a district, and to report to the Central Government on the complicated affairs with which he has to deal, must be a man of a great deal of education.

3. But it happens that the only race in India which readily acquires the kind of education necessary for governing according to a civilised and progressive standard is that of the Bengalees—the inhabitants of the Province of Bengal.

4. **Governing by Natives would mean Governing by Bengalee Baboos.**—If, then, we ruled India entirely by native Indians, we should be forced to employ what are called Bengalee Baboos, that is, educated Bengalees. But, unfortunately, the Bengalee Baboos are exceedingly unpopular with the majority

of the people of India. They are despised as being weak, cowardly, and effeminate, and are generally looked down upon by the rest of the natives of India. This feeling is very likely most unfair, and is of course to be regretted, but our regret cannot alter the plain fact. The Bengalee Baboos are also, as a rule, Hindus, and therefore disliked by the Mohammedans. Add to this the fact, that outside their own Province of Bengal they are as much foreigners as Englishmen. The peasantry of the Punjab would consider a Bengalee Baboo quite as great a stranger to them as an Englishman. They would understand his language no better, and would have very little more sympathy with his ways of thought. On the whole, then, it is less unfair to put Englishmen over the people of an Indian district than to put a native who would probably only be welcomed by one section of its inhabitants.

5. **The Sense of Duty.**—There is yet another reason why Englishmen govern India better than natives. Englishmen unquestionably have the sense of duty more highly developed, are more capable of self-sacrifice, are more just and impartial, and generally have a wider and better idea as to what is due to the governed from the governor than have natives. The native may be after his own way a very good man, but he is a fatalist, and he is without the energy of the European—the energy which makes men restless till they find remedies for wrongs. The native, face to face with a disaster or an act of oppression, will fold his hands and conclude that it is the will of God that things should go wrong. "Without doubt what *is* is right." That is the common feeling of the

Asiatic. The Englishman, on the other hand, feels that nothing is so wrong that it cannot be remedied, or so good that it cannot be improved.

6. **The Best possible Government for India is English Government.**—It is, then, quite clear that if we are to give India the best possible government we must continue to govern that great continent by means of Englishmen. This does not, of course, mean that we are to exclude the Indians from all share in the work of government. It merely means that we must keep, not only the central control in the hands of Englishmen, but the supreme control in each district. All the subordinate work can be done as well and more cheaply by natives, but the last word on every important question, as long as we remain in India, should be spoken by Englishmen. This is, in fact, the rule on which India has been and is governed at the present moment.

7. **The Native Element in the Indian Government.**—The general work of government is done by many thousands of native officials, but controlling and supervising them is a small number of Englishmen. Of these there are at the present moment less than 1000. It must not be supposed, however, that this arrangement shuts out the natives altogether from the highest posts. If a native shows himself capable of exceptional governing power he may be raised to the highest judicial office, or he may become a member of the Legislative Council which helps to govern India. The present arrangement, then, is probably the best that could be devised for giving good government to India. It secures impartiality and energy in the administration, and a civilised standard of govern-

ment, and at the same time gives employment to a large number of the natives of India.

8. There are in India 114,150 civil appointments worth more than £10 a year each. Of these 97 in each hundred are held by natives, and only 3 in each hundred by Englishmen.

8. *Impartiality.* Perfect fairness.

Chapter XV

1. **The Government of India.**—The government of India is placed in the hands of a Governor-General or Viceroy, who is appointed by the Government at home, and so indirectly by the people of the United Kingdom. Nominally his powers are almost unlimited, but as a matter of fact his actions are largely controlled by the Secretary of State for India, who is a member of the British Ministry. On all important questions and on new departures in policy advice is asked from the Secretary of State, and that advice is followed. For example, no fresh territory would ever be annexed without the consent of the Secretary of State for India. The Governor-General has, to help him in the work of Government, two Councils. One of these, called the Council, consists of the heads of the various Indian departments, and is very much like the Cabinet Council at home—the Governor-General being like the Sovereign and Prime Minister rolled into one.

2. **The Legislative Council.**—Besides this there is the Legislative Council, which is a sort of Parliament in which laws are discussed and passed. This

AL HILLA, FROM THE SUSPENSION BRIDGE, LOOKING NORTH-WEST

Council is made up of the heads of the departments of State, and a certain number of other members, some nominated by the Government, and some chosen by native bodies, as their representatives. The Legislative Council thus contains a certain number of natives, and their opinions on new laws are found most valuable.

3. **Governors and Lieutenant - Governors.** — Under the Governor-General are the Governors, Lieutenant-Governors, and Commissioners of the various provinces into which India is divided. The Governors of the two great provinces of Madras and Bombay, and the Lieutenant-Governor of Bengal, have also Councils and Legislative Councils to help them in the work of law-making and governing.

4. **The District.**—The provinces and commissionerships are again divided into districts, and at the head of each district is an officer, who is usually a European. Under him are a great many native officials, and one or two young Englishmen who are learning the work of government.

5. **The Indian Army.**—The Government keep in India a large number of English troops, generally about 70,000 men. Besides these there is what is called the native army. This consists of cavalry and infantry recruited among the warlike natives of India. But though the rank and file are natives, the greater part of the officers, and all those of superior rank, are English. The Indian army contains many splendid regiments, and on various occasions has been of use to England outside India. For example, Indian troops helped us in Egypt and in Abyssinia. If India were to be invaded the Indian army would prove of the greatest possible service.

6. The main use of both the English and the native troops in India is to keep the peace, and to prevent the fierce and brave, but only half-civilised races which inhabit great parts of India fighting among each other. This they would most certainly do but for the presence of our armies. There are a dozen races and chiefs and rajahs who each consider that they have a right to hold all India, and, if we did not prevent them by the fear of our forces, would try and conquer the whole peninsula. This keeping of the peace in India is the greatest of all the many benefits conferred on the Indians by British rule.

7. **The Native States.**—Included within India are a large number of states governed by native princes, but controlled to a larger or greater extent by the Indian Government. These native princes are what is called Feudatories of the British Empire. They cannot, that is, make war or peace by themselves, or have any dealings with foreign powers, or with each other; but within their own dominions they can do pretty much as they like, provided always that they do not oppress their people by too much taxation, or in other ways rule badly or tyrannically.

8. **When shall we be able to leave India to govern itself?**—This is a question which people often ask. The true answer is, When India is fit to do so. And when will that be? When India has become a homogeneous people. When a long course of good government and the careful preservation of the peace has taught the people of India to think of themselves as one country, and has taken away from the different races the desire to fight with and conquer each other, our work will have been accomplished,

and we shall be able to depart in peace. Till then, we must train the people in the ways of good government, and teach them to understand its value. At present they do not understand it, and look upon all we have done and are doing for them as not worth accomplishing. In all probability it will take more than another hundred years to weld the peoples of India together, and make them capable of self-government.

9. **"No Hurrying" should be our Rule in India.**—This being so, we must be in no hurry, but must steadily and quietly press forward in the task of good government—always remembering that our duty is not to make ourselves popular with the Indians, but to give them the best and most just government possible. If we remember that, and recognise that India has been given to us by Providence as a trust, we cannot go far wrong. When, then, any new scheme is proposed for governing India our duty is plain. It is to find out whether the change will really be for the good of India, and if it will be, to adopt it: if not, to reject it. This, and this only, is the path of safety.

VI.—CONCLUSION

Chapter XVI

1. **Our Duty to the Empire.**—Before we leave the subject of the Empire we will quote the eloquent words in which Lord Rosebery has summed up the duties of the citizen in regard to the Empire.

2. After reminding us that we inhabit an Empire, not an island, Lord Rosebery proceeds:—

There are few political facts, perhaps none, that should exercise so great an influence on their future lives.

For a collection of states spread over every region of the earth, but owning one head and one flag, is even more important as an influence than as an Empire. From either point of view it is a world-wide fact of supreme significance; but in the one capacity it affects only its own subjects, and in the other all mankind. With the Empire statesmen are mainly concerned; in the influence every individual can and must have a part. Influence is based on character, and it is on the character of each child that grows into manhood within British limits that the future of our Empire rests.

If we and they are narrow and selfish, averse to labour, impatient of necessary burdens, factious and self-indulgent; if we see in public affairs not our Empire but our country, not our country but our parish, and in our parish our house, the Empire is doomed. For its maintenance requires work and sacrifice and intelligence.

If, on the other hand, we aim at the diffusion of the blessings of industry undisturbed by war, if we aim at peace secured, not by humiliation but preponderance, we need to preserve our Empire not for ourselves only but for mankind. And this is said not pharisaically, not to the exclusion of other countries, but because ours is the most widely spread and the most penetrating of nationalities. The time, indeed, cannot be far remote when the British Empire must, if it remain united, by the growth of its population and its ubiquitous dominion, exercise a controlling authority in the world. To that trust our sons are born.

I hope, then, that the youth of our race will learn . . . how great is their inheritance and their responsibility. Those outside these islands may learn the splendour of their source and their "home," as well as communion with the other regions under the Crown of Great Britain; and within, English, Scottish, and Irish children may learn not to be shut in their shires, but that they are the heirs of great responsibilities and a vast inheritance. History has marked those that made this Empire, and will mark, with equal certainty, but in a different spirit, those who unmake it or allow it to dissolve.[1]

3. **The Union Jack.**—When men die fighting for their country they are buried wrapt in the English flag—the Union Jack; and this honour is extended to those who have served their country well in other ways. When the poet Tennyson was buried in Westminster Abbey his coffin was covered with a Union Jack, because it was felt that he deserved the gratitude and respect of the whole nation. The Union Jack represents to men's minds the might, majesty, and honour

---

[1] See Preface contributed by Lord Rosebery to Mr. Parkin's *Round the Empire* (Cassell and Co.).

of England and of the English-speaking race within the Empire.

4. It is well, then, to understand the origin and various forms of the flag of England. The flag of England, usually called the Union Jack, shows the respective national crosses of the three Kingdoms of England, Scotland, and Ireland. It should properly be called the Union Flag, but the name Union Jack has come to be commonly used from ships displaying from a staff at the end of the bowsprit a Union Flag *as a*

Jack — the name given to the small flag flown at the bowsprit. The blue field, or ground of the Union flag, is the field of the flag of Scotland, both England and Ireland having white fields on their national flags. The red cross of St. George is placed on the blue field in the Union flag, with a narrow line of white separating the red cross from the blue field, since to put two colours one on the top of the other, "colour on colour," is bad heraldry.

5. The two saltires (or X-shaped crosses) of St. Andrew and St. Patrick cross the Union flag diagonally.

The saltire of St. Andrew is white and the saltire of St. Patrick is red; the red and white are placed alternately uppermost, the narrow line of white being placed, for the same reason as stated above, wherever the red saltire would touch the blue ground. Once more, then, the Union Jack consists of three crosses on a blue ground: the red cross of St. George, the white saltire or X-shaped cross of St. Andrew, and the red saltire of St. Patrick—the two last being placed alternately uppermost. A narrow line of white separates the red cross and the red saltire from the blue ground wherever these would touch each other.

6. The flag, with a large field and a small Union flag in the upper corner next the staff, which is erected over the poop of a British vessel or flown from the gaff when she is under sail, is called the Ensign. There are three Ensigns—the Red, White, and Blue. The Red, consisting of a red field and a small Union flag in the top left-hand corner, belongs to merchant ships, passenger steamers, and generally to all vessels not belonging to the navy. It is, therefore, the flag most generally seen.

7. The flag which belongs to the navy is the White Ensign; that is the national flag of England, the red cross of St. George on a white field, with a Union flag in the same place as in the Red Ensign (the top left-hand corner). This flag is also used by the Royal Yacht Squadron. The Blue Ensign, a blue field with a Union flag in the usual place, is borne by vessels of the Naval Reserve, and also by the ships of certain Yacht Clubs. It will thus be seen that the national colours of the United Kingdom are red, white, and blue—colours which we share with our brothers the Americans, whose flag originally consisted of a field of alternate

red and white stripes with the British Union flag, without the cross of St. Patrick, as it was before the Union with Ireland, in the familiar place in the top left-hand corner.

8. After the Declaration of Independence America superseded the British Union flag in the corner with a device of thirteen white stars (the then number of States) on a blue field. A new star has been added for each new State, so that America's flag now consists of a ground of thirteen white and red stripes, and in the top left-hand corner a blue field with as many white stars upon it as there are States. This is the famous flag of the stars and stripes,—a flag second only in interest to Englishmen to the national flag, the Union Jack of Great Britain and Ireland. The other English flags are the Royal Standard and the flag of the Admiralty, a red field with a gold anchor and cable on it. The Lord-Lieutenant of Ireland flies the Union flag with a blue shield in the centre with a gold harp on it, and the Governor-General of India the Union flag, with the Star of India with a crown over it within the centre. British Colonies fly the Blue Ensign with the badge of the Colony on the fly or edge farthest from the staff.

9. The Union Jack should be honoured and loved by all of us, as it is the flag of our country, and reminds us of all we hold most dear. People sometimes say, What does a piece of bunting with stripes on it matter? It is childish to love and revere a piece of calico or linen. Those who talk thus talk nonsense. We do not, of course, revere and love the piece of bunting or the stripes, but what they represent—that is our country. The Union Jack is a symbol of the union which binds

Englishmen all the world over. A poet, Mr. Rudyard Kipling, in a beautiful and stirring ballad, has told us what the flag of England means, and how it passes over every sea and ocean, and is everywhere the sign of England.

10. The poet asks, What is the flag of England? and the four winds of heaven answer him, and tell what has been dared and done under the flag of England. The North wind tells how the flag has flown among the storms, and ice, and darkness of the frozen seas—

The lean white bear hath seen it in the long, long arctic night,
The musk-ox knows the standard that flouts the northern light:
What is the flag of England? Ye have but my bergs to dare,
Ye have but my drifts to conquer. Go forth, for it is there.

11. The South wind tells how in every part of the world the English flag is flying—

I have wrenched it free from the halliard to hang for a wisp on the Horn;
I have chased it north to the Lizard—ribboned and rolled and torn;
I have spread its fold o'er the dying adrift in a hopeless sea;
I have hurled it swift on the slaver, and seen the slave set free.

12. The East wind tells how even the deserts and mountains of Asia know the flag—

The desert dust hath dimmed it, the flying wild-ass knows,
The scared white leopard winds it across the taintless snows.
What is the flag of England? Ye have but my sun to dare,
Ye have but my sands to travel. Go forth, for it is there.

P

13. The West wind tells how in the wildest weather and fiercest storms—

Dipping between the rollers, the English flag goes by.

And how—

The dead dumb fog hath wrapped it—the frozen dews have kissed,
The naked stars have seen it, a fellow-star in the mist.

14. This noble poem should remind us how worldwide is the flag of England, and how in an exact sense Englishmen are citizens of the world. As Dryden said long ago, we are not prisoners to our isle, but wherever the four winds of heaven blow there is a piece of England covered by the English flag.

Chapter XVII

The United States

1. **America.** — We have dealt with our duties towards the Empire. We must now say something about those towards foreign countries. Before doing so, however, we must speak of a nation which no right-feeling Englishmen will ever call foreign. That nation is the United States of America. It is peopled by men of our blood and faith, enjoys in a great measure the same laws as we do, reads the same Bible, and acknowledges like us the rule of King Shakespeare.

2. **How we lost America.** — At one time

the United States consisted of English colonies, but about 120 years ago the Government foolishly tried to interfere with the colonists, and would not allow them to have control over their own affairs. Accordingly the men of the New England on the other side of the Atlantic determined to set up for themselves, and after a fierce struggle became independent. This unhappy war for a long time left bitter memories, but now (God be thanked) the English on both sides of the Atlantic have become good friends again. Though we must ever deeply regret that the American English should have parted from us in anger, we cannot but feel that their country has become so vast that it probably would have been necessary for them in any case to establish a separate government.

3. All, then, that we need be sorry for is that the two halves of the English-speaking race did not part in kindness, and did not agree that in some form or other they would acknowledge before the whole world that their people were brethren and not strangers. But though the war of a hundred years ago made this acknowledgment of an essential brotherhood impossible for many years, there is no reason why in the time to come it should not be accomplished.

4. It would be quite possible for the people of the British Empire and of the United States to enter upon an agreement, placing their relations on a footing quite different from that which belongs to foreign states, and acknowledging thereby their common origin. Some day this will doubtless be accomplished. Till it is every English-speaking man, woman, and child should look forward to the event and do his best to bring it

about. Let us remember, then, that the United States is not and never can be in reality a foreign country, nor an American a foreigner. They and we are one flesh.

5. **Foreign Countries.** — But though we must reserve for our brethren in the United States a special feeling of love and sympathy, we must not forget to maintain as friendly a feeling as possible towards those countries which are rightly called foreign countries, such as France, Italy, Russia, Germany. It is our duty to think of all foreigners with kindliness, and never to allow ourselves to be led into the silly error of thinking that certain nations are our "natural enemies." We must not think that because foreigners have different forms of government, different customs and different religions, that they are in any way inferior or to be despised. Their institutions are their business, not ours, and we have no right to interfere with them. This, however, will not prevent us from sympathising with the best elements in each nation, and hoping that they will prevail. There is nothing unfriendly or unwise in wishing a foreign country the happiness of good government.

6. **Justice in International Arrangements.** — Nations, like individuals, find it impossible to live in isolation. They constantly have to settle questions among each other. Now it is essential for the good citizen to remember that it is the duty of the nation to which he belongs to behave justly and fairly, and to make no attempt to deceive or get the better of other nations by underhand means.

7. A nation, in transacting international business, should behave as does an honourable and self-

respecting man in private life. Like him it should hold firmly to its just rights, and like him it should be moderate, reasonable, and fair in dealing with the rights of others. We should never do as a nation what we should be ashamed of doing as men. For example, we should never let a foolish sense of pride prevent us owning ourselves in the wrong if we are in the wrong, nor should we allow bad faith in a foreign nation to be an excuse for bad faith on our part. We do not make stealing or lying in other people an excuse for stealing or lying ourselves.

8. **International Courtesy.**—Especially ought we to treat foreign nations with politeness and courtesy. Foreigners are naturally apt to misunderstand us and we them, and therefore we should be specially careful in regard to the way in which we speak of foreigners and their customs. People who laugh at foreigners and abuse foreign countries usually do so from ignorance, and without meaning any real offence, but it constantly happens that they do a great deal of harm, and make foreigners imagine that all English people are brutal and discourteous. We ought then to make a special effort to show ourselves courteous and kindly to foreign nations.

9. We ought, too, each one of us, to try and change the bad old system under which foreign countries were regarded as necessarily hostile, and were expected to hate each other out of a sort of evil custom, and because they had always hated each other. If we are told that the people of this or that foreign country hate us that is no reason for hating them. Rather it is a reason for trying to get the better of their hate by trying to treat

them with more than ordinary courtesy, justice, and right feeling.

10. **The whole Duty of the Citizen.**—The whole duty of the citizen at home and abroad may be summed up in a few words. It is to be a patriot or lover of his country; but to be, as Burke said, a patriot in such a way as not to forget that he is a gentleman—that is, a man just, kindly, honourable, courteous, and self-respecting. At home the citizen shows his love of his country by trying to develop his talents of mind and body to the best possible advantage, and by trying to raise the moral standard of those among whom he lives. In the Empire, by maintaining friendship and brotherhood with his English kinsmen beyond sea, and by giving the best possible government to those countries which, like India, are peopled by the various coloured races which have proved less capable of civilisation and progress. Abroad, by treating all foreign countries with moderation, justice, and good faith. It is no doubt difficult in practice to do all these things, but the good citizen is he whose actions come nearest to the ideal.

MAP OF BRITISH POSSESSIONS

APPENDIX A

The Factory Acts

It is of importance that the workers should understand clearly the nature of the Acts of Parliament made to protect their interests; and we will therefore give an abstract of the various Acts, drawn from the excellent book on the Factory and Workshop Acts compiled by Mr. Alexander and Mr. Jasper A. Redgrave (Shaw and Sons, Fetter Lane). It must first be noticed, however, that up till 1878 there were a great number of laws regulating factories and workshops. In that year an Act was passed combining them into one. Since then (in 1891) another Act was passed on the subject. The provisions of both these Acts are included in the following summary of the chief regulations to be observed in Factories, Works, Mills, and Workshops:[1]—

SANITARY PROVISIONS

Every factory to be kept clean, well ventilated, not overcrowded.

If an inspector observe a nuisance he must report to sanitary authority.

---

[1] In this list the Regulations in the Textile Trades are taken as the basis, and only the important differences in the non-Textile Trades are noticed. The minor points of divergence are ignored, and a number of technical and less important restrictions are altogether omitted in order to save space.

Every factory to be limewashed once in 14 months, unless painted in oil once in seven years, when it must be washed once every 14 months.

A child, young person, or woman not to be employed in wet spinning, unless means are taken to prevent their being wetted, and to prevent the escape of steam.

Where dirt is generated by grinding, glazing, or polishing, a fan is to be provided to prevent inhalation of dust.

Bakehouses to be limewashed once in six months.

PROVISIONS AS TO SAFETY

Dangerous machinery to be securely fenced.

Employment of a child in cleaning machinery in motion, and of a child, young person, or woman in cleaning mill gearing in motion, prohibited.

Employment between fixed and traversing parts of a self-acting machine forbidden.

Notice of accidents to be sent to the inspector and certifying surgeon—If fatal, or if caused by machinery moved by power, or vat or pan, and so as to prevent the injured person returning to his work for five hours on three days after the accident.

If any person suffer bodily injury from machinery, etc., required to be fenced, but not fenced, the occupier is liable to a penalty of £100, which may be applied by the Secretary of State for the benefit of the injured person.

Sufficient means of escape from fire to be provided in the case of factories.

EMPLOYMENT AND MEALS

Young Persons

The period of employment, inclusive of meal hours, shall be either between 6 A.M. and 6 P.M., or between 7 A.M. and 7 P.M.

APPENDIX A

On Saturday, when work commences at 6 A.M.,—

If not less than one hour be given for meals, manufacturing processes must cease at 1 P.M., and all other work at 1.30 P.M.

If less than one hour be given for meals, manufacturing processes must cease at 12.30 P.M., and all other work at 1 P.M.

On Saturday, when work commences at 7 A.M., manufacturing processes must cease at 1.30 P.M., and all other work at 2 P.M.

If the occupier of a factory be of the Jewish religion, and close his factory on Saturday until sunset, he can employ young persons and women until 9 P.M. on Saturday.

All young persons and women must have two hours for meals during the period of employment, of which one hour must be given before 3 P.M.

On Saturday, at least half an hour must be given.

A young person or woman not to be employed for more than four hours and a half without an interval of half an hour.

CHILDREN

Children are to be employed either morning or afternoon, or on alternate days.

The period of employment for a child begins and ends the same as for a young person.

Children in the morning set must cease work at the dinner hour, but not later than 1 P.M.

Children in the afternoon set begin at the end of the dinner-time, but not later than 1 P.M.

Children may work on the alternate day system on Saturdays as young persons.

A child shall not be employed on Saturday in two successive weeks, nor on Saturday in any week, if on any other day in the week he has worked more than five hours and a half.

Children working on alternate days may work as young persons, but must not work on two successive days, nor on the same days in two successive weeks.

When a child is employed as a young person, he must have the same intervals for meals as a young person.

A child not to be employed more than four hours and a half without an interval of half an hour :—Except

In the factories named in Sched. 3, Part 2, and others added thereto by the Secretary of State.

HOLIDAYS

Every child, young person, and woman shall be allowed the following holidays :—

The whole of Christmas Day and the whole of Good Friday ; or instead of Good Friday the next public holiday under the Holidays Extension Act, 1875.

Notice must be given of such holidays and fixed up in the factory.

A half holiday shall comprise one-half of the period of employment on some other day than Saturday.

A child, young person, or woman shall not be employed on any day or part of a day set apart for a holiday.

In Scotland, other days may be substituted for Christmas Day and Good Friday.

Eight half-holidays or equivalent whole holidays, of which half shall be given between 15th March and 1st October following.

In the factory of a Jew, in which all the persons employed are Jews, two Bank Holidays may be given instead of Christmas Day and Good Friday.

In Ireland, the 17th of March, or Good Friday or Easter Tuesday, must be given, and will reckon as two of the eight half-holidays.

APPENDIX A

REGULATIONS AS TO MEAL TIMES

All children, young persons, and women to have the times allowed for meals at the same periods of the day.

A child, young person, or woman is not allowed to remain in any room where a manufacturing process is being carried on, or to be employed during a meal time.

Meals not to be taken in certain parts of glass-works, lucifer-match works, and earthenware works.

Notice of meal hours to be fixed up.

PROHIBITIONS OF EMPLOYMENT

A child shall not be employed under the age of eleven years.

A child, young person, or woman shall not be employed on Sunday ; but

If the occupier be of the Jewish religion, and close his factory on Saturday, both before and after sunset, a Jewish young person or woman may be employed on Sunday the same as if Sunday were Saturday.

A child or young person is not to be employed in the silvering of mirrors by the mercurial process, or the making of white lead.

A child or female young person is not to be employed in melting or annealing glass.

A female under sixteen is not to be employed in brick-making or salt-making.

A child is not to be employed in dry grinding in the metal trades, or where lucifer-match dipping is carried on.

A child under eleven shall not be employed in metal-grinding, other than dry metal grinding, or in fustian cutting.

MISCELLANEOUS REGULATIONS

Notice to be hung up of times of work and meals, also abstract of Act and names of inspectors and certifying surgeons.

Hours of work to be regulated by a public clock.

Any person in a factory while machinery is in motion or while a manufacturing process is carried on deemed to be employed, unless the contrary be proved.

It should be noted that a child is a person under the age of fourteen, a young person a person between fourteen and eighteen, and a woman a person above eighteen.

APPENDIX B

THE LABOUR DEPARTMENT MEMORANDUM

Official Memorandum under which the Labour Department of the Board of Trade was established :—

1. A *Labour Gazette* will be issued, at first monthly, but perhaps more frequently hereafter. Its object will be to supply accurate information on subjects of special interest to workmen and workwomen. Thus Mr. Burnett's monthly reports on the state of the skilled labour market will appear in a more fully developed form in the *Gazette*. There will be also an account of trade disputes begun, closed, or in progress during the month, and of important industrial negotiations, such as arbitrations, changes of sliding scales, apportionment of work between different trades, etc.

A monthly digest will be published of reports from factory and mines' inspectors to the Home Office on the state of labour in their districts, so far as it comes within their province; on accidents, proceedings under the Factory and Workshop Acts, the Mines Regulation Acts; and it is hoped, so far as practicable, to refer to important proceedings under the Employers' Liability Act; to action taken by Local Authorities with regard to the sanitary condition of workshops, and by Local Authorities under the Acts bearing on the housing of the poor. Important meetings and conferences, *e.g.* the Trades Union and Co-operative Congresses, meetings of the Miners' Federation, international congresses on labour questions, etc., will be noticed.

It is proposed to obtain from the Chief Registrar of

Friendly Societies a monthly account of all Trade Unions workmen's Co-operative Societies, and Friendly Societie registered or dissolved during the month.

It is hoped, by arrangement with the Board of Agri culture, and otherwise, to obtain for the *Gazette*, fron time to time, particulars as to the working of the Acts fo providing allotments and small holdings, and other matter bearing on the condition of agricultural labour.

At frequent intervals, reports on matters speciall; affecting women's labour will be prepared for the *Gazett* by the Lady Labour Correspondent. An effort will b made to supplement the report of the Chief Labour Cor respondent on the state of the skilled labour market, b; obtaining each month accurate particulars as to changes ii volume of employment in certain irregular trades, *e.g* (possibly London dock labour in continuation of th inquiry completed for the Royal Commission on Labou by Mr. Charles Booth). Besides treating of these an similar special labour subjects, it is hoped to give statistic in the *Gazette* on such subjects as pauperism, saving banks, education (especially in its industrial aspects) exports and imports, and the retail price level of the chie articles of ordinary consumption by workmen, as well a comparative tables of wholesale prices of leading article in the chief markets of the world. Notices will be inserte of the more important events affecting labour in variou foreign countries; and a list will be periodically publishe of Government publications, both in the United Kingdon and abroad, which treat of labour matters, with a shor popular abstract of the contents of the more important o these documents, and of important legislation at hom and abroad, passed from time to time, having an importan bearing on labour.

The *Labour Gazette* will be published at 1d., and a larg number of copies will be gratuitously distributed to fre libraries, workmen's organisations, mechanics' institutes chambers of commerce, and other institutions.

2. Special inquiries will be undertaken from time t

time by the Labour Department into important subjects bearing on labour on which adequate information is not at present available. Among the subjects requiring such special inquiries which the Department hopes to enter upon shortly are :—

(*a*) The amount and causes of fluctuations of employment in certain seasonal and irregular trades, and their effects on the conditions and efficiency of the labour employed;

(*b*) An account of actual attempts made in the United Kingdom or abroad to relieve distress by providing public work either by relief works, municipal or national workshops, farm colonies or the like, and the causes of their failure or success;

(*c*) Certain questions bearing on the conditions of child employment both in and out of factories and workshops;

(*d*) An account of the effects on labour of noxious processes in use in certain typical groups of unhealthy trades, *e.g.* potteries, white lead works, cutlery, chemicals, etc., treated so far as practicable both from the statistical and the scientific and medical points of view.

Other important matters which may also probably demand special inquiries are the economic effects of alien immigration, various methods of wage payment and adjustment (*e.g.* sliding scales, profit-sharing, co-operation, etc.), work of married women, cost of living, hours of labour, overtime, etc.

3. The Department also will be prepared to carry out such special inquiries as may be ordered from time to time by Parliament into labour questions.

4. The Department hopes to publish an Annual Report of its proceedings, framed, as far as possible, so as to be a handy book of reference for workmen to the principal labour questions which have engaged the attention of the Department during the year.

APPENDIX C

List of British Possessions

The Roll-Call of the Empire.—Here is a full list of all the British Possessions in India and elsewhere. They may be traced out on the map at the end of this volume.

NOTE.—The following list is based upon one prepared for paper by Lord Thring on the Consolidation of the British Empire, published in *The Scottish Geographical Magazine*. The list was revised by Mr. J. R. Fitzgerald of the Imperial Institute.

EUROPE

United Kingdom of Great Britain and Ireland

ISLE OF MAN.
CHANNEL ISLANDS.
GIBRALTAR.
MALTA, GOZO, AND COMINO.

ASIA

Indian Empire

BENGAL AND NATIVE STATES.[1]
N.W. PROVINCES, AND OUDH AND NATIVE STATES.[1]
PUNJAB AND NATIVE STATES.[1]
ASSAM.
AJMERE AND MERWARA.
MADRAS AND NATIVE STATES.[1]
Laccadive Islands.
BOMBAY AND NATIVE STATES.[1]
CENTRAL PROVINCES & NATIVE STATES.[1]

---

[1] These Native States are under these respective governments, in contradistinction to those included below under the separate heading of Native States.

APPENDIX C

ERAR.
OORG.
OWER BURMAH.
PPER BURMAH.
BRITISH BALUCHISTAN.
ANDAMAN AND NICOBAR ISLANDS.

Native States

Rajputana Agency.
Central India Agency.
Baroda.
Haidarabad.
Mysore.
Kashmir.
Sikkim.
Manipur.
Tribes East of Assam.
Lushai and Kachin.
Shan States.
Baluchistan Agency.
Indo-Afghan Frontier.

ADEN.
   Perim.
   Socotra.
   Kuria Muria Islands.
CEYLON.
   Maldive Islands.
BAHREIN ISLANDS.
KAMARAN ISLANDS.
CYPRUS.
STRAITS SETTLEMENTS.
   Christmas Island.
   Keeling Island.
MALAY PROTECTORATES.
   Perak, Selangor, Sungei-Ujong, Jelebu, and Negri-Sembilan.
   Johore and Pahang.
   The Dindings.
NORTH BORNEO.
BRUNEI.
SARAWAK.
LABUAN.
SPRATTLEY ISLAND and Amboyna Cay.
HONG KONG.

AFRICA

AMBIA.
SIERRA LEONE.
GOLD COAST.
LAGOS.
NIGER PROTECTORATE.
OIL RIVERS PROTECTORATE.
BRITISH EAST AFRICA.
SOMAL LAND.
ZANZIBAR.
CAPE COLONY.
   Basutoland.
   Bechuanaland.
   Zambesia and Nyassaland.

NATAL.
   Zululand.
MAURITIUS.
   Rodriguez, and Cargados Garajos.
   Seychelles.
   Amirante Islands.
   Chagos and Oil Islands.
ASCENSION.
ST. HELENA.
   Tristan da Cunha, Inaccessible, Nightingale, and Gough's Island.

AMERICA

DOMINION OF CANADA.
   Ontario.
   Quebec.
   Nova Scotia.
   New Brunswick.
   Prince Edward Island.
   Manitoba.
   North-West Territories
   British Columbia.

THE CITIZEN AND THE STATE

NEWFOUNDLAND.
    Labrador.
BRITISH HONDURAS.
BERMUDA ISLANDS.
THE BAHAMAS.
JAMAICA.
    Turk's and Caicos Islands.
    Cayman Islands.
    Pedro and Morant Cays.
LEEWARD ISLANDS.
    Antigua.
    Barbuda and Redonda.
    Virgin Islands.
    Dominica.
    St. Kitt's, Nevis, and Anguilla.
    Montserrat.
    Sombrero (*Virgin Is.*)
WINDWARD ISLANDS.
    Grenada, and part of Gr
      dines.
    St. Lucia, and part of Gr
      dines.
    St. Vincent.
BARBADOS.
TRINIDAD.
    Tobago.
BRITISH GUIANA.
FALKLAND ISLANDS.
    South Georgia.

AUSTRALASIA

NEW SOUTH WALES.
    Lord Howe Island.
    Norfolk Island.
    Pitcairn Island.
VICTORIA.
SOUTH AUSTRALIA.
    Northern Territory.
QUEENSLAND.
    British New Guinea.
WESTERN AUSTRALIA.
TASMANIA.
NEW ZEALAND.
    Chatham Islands.
    Kermadec Islands.
    Bounty Island.
    Antipodes Islands.
    Auckland Islands.
    Macquarie Islands.
FIJI ISLANDS.
    Rotumah Island.
PACIFIC ISLANDS.
    Fanning Island.
    Christmas Island.
    Malden Island.
    Starbuck Island.
    Tongarewa (Penrhyn) Is.
    Manihiki Islands.
    Suvaroff Islands.
    Union Islands.
    Phœnix Islands.
    Cook's Islands.
    Caroline Island.
    Ellice Islands.
    Washington Island.
    Jarvis Island.
    Dudoza Island.
    Savage Island.
    Royal Company Island.
    Ducie Island.
    Emerald Island.
    Campbell Island.

THE END

Printed by R. & R. CLARK, *Edinburgh.*

SCHEDULE I.

MACMILLAN'S NEW LITERARY READERS.

An entirely new and important Series of Reading Books for the Use of Elementary Schools.

These books have been compiled by exceptionally competent educational authorities, and possess a distinctive feature above all other series in the market, inasmuch as the volumes for the Middle and Higher Classes are almost exclusively composed of copyright matter of a high literary character.

The authors drawn upon for the purposes of compilation include Lord Tennyson, Kingsley, Christina Rossetti, Matthew Arnold, Thomas Hughes, Lewis Carroll, Charlotte Yonge, Archibald Forbes, Sir Archibald Geikie, Professor Freeman, Stopford Brooke, and many others.

The extracts have been carefully chosen and graded, and the volumes are provided with full and ample annotations. They are strongly bound and lavishly illustrated throughout; the Primers and Infant Reader being supplied with numerous coloured illustrations.

Primer I. (32 pp.)	4d.	
" II. (48 pp.)	4d.	
Infant Reader (72 pp.)	6d.	*In the Press.*
Reader I. (112 pp.)	8d.	
" II. (128 pp.)	10d.	*In preparation.*
" III. (176 pp.)	1s.	
" IV. (208 pp.)	1s. 3d.	*Ready.*
" V. (240 pp.)	1s. 6d.	
" VI. (256 pp.)	1s. 6d.	*In the Press.*

MACMILLAN'S HISTORY READERS.

Globe 8vo. Illustrated.

Adopted by the London, Bradford, Bristol, Cardiff, Edinburgh, Edmonton, Halifax, Huddersfield, Leeds, Manchester, Newcastle-on-Tyne, Northampton, Norwich, Nottingham, Portsmouth, Reading, Southampton, Swansea, Swindon, Tottenham, West Ham, and other School Boards.

Book I. (*In the Press.*)	
Book II. Simple Stories from English History	10d.
Book III. Stories and Tales from Early History	1s.
Book IV. Stories and Biographies, 1066 to 1485	1s. 3d.
Book V. The Tudor Period	1s. 6d.
Book VI. The Stuart Period	1s. 6d.
Book VII. The Hanoverian Period	1s. 6d.

MACMILLAN AND CO., LONDON.

SCHEDULE I.—*Continued.*

MACMILLAN'S SCIENCE READERS.

For the use of Elementary Schools. By V. T. MURCHÉ, Head Master of Boundary Lane Board School, Camberwell. In Six Books. [*Ready Shortly*

> Book I. . . . . 1s.
> ,, II. . . . . 1s.
> ,, III. . . . . 1s. 4d.
> ,, IV. . . . . 1s. 4d.
> ,, V. . . . . 1s. 6d.
> ,, VI. . . . . 1s. 6d.

VARIED OCCUPATIONS IN WEAVING. By LOUISA WALKER, Head Mistress (Infants') Fleet Road Board School, Hampstead. With Illustrations. Crown 8vo. [*Ready in January.*

A Teachers' Text-book of "Practical Kindergarten for Schools," and "suitable occupations" for Infants and Lower Standards, based upon the Froëbelian principles of training the "Hand and Eye;" with the application of the same to the construction of useful articles.

The book treats on various kinds of weaving—horizontal, diagonal, open, free and fancy—in paper, ribbon, string, straw and cane.

Chair-caning and straw-plait are dealt with, and full details of the methods employed, and materials necessary, are given for each occupation.

UPPER STANDARD READERS.

THE CITIZEN AND THE STATE. Reading Books for Elementary Schools.

> PART I. Representative Government. By E. J. MATHEW, M.A., LL.B. Globe 8vo. 1s. 6d.
>
> PART II. Industrial and Social Life, and the Empire. By J. ST. LOE STRACHEY. Globe 8vo. 1s. 6d.

THE ENGLISH CITIZEN ; HIS LIFE AND DUTIES. By CHARLES HENRY WYATT, Clerk of the Manchester School Board. With about 100 illustrations. 256 pages. Globe 8vo. 2s.

A Text-book for Evening Continuation Schools, and the Higher Standards in Elementary Schools.

* This book is drawn up in accordance with the directions given in the New Code for Evening Continuation Schools.

MACMILLAN AND CO., LONDON.

SCHEDULE I.—Continued.

MACMILLAN'S SCHOOL EDITIONS OF COPYRIGHT STANDARD WORKS.

Prepared for use as Reading Books in the Upper Classes of Elementary Schools. The Books are abridged by the omission of difficult passages, but the author's text is not otherwise interfered with. Globe 8vo, well illustrated, 1s. 6d. each.

THE LANCES OF LYNWOOD. By CHARLOTTE M. YONGE. Abridged Edition for Schools. With Illustrations. Globe 8vo. 1s. 6d.

EDUCATIONAL TIMES.—"The abridgment required to bring the book down to the limits of a Reader is the work of a skilful and intelligent hand."

GLASGOW HERALD.—"*The Lances of Lynwood* is an excellent abridgment, for use in advanced classes, of Charlotte M. Yonge's thrilling story of the reign of King Edward the Third. A brief introduction, with a map and a genealogical table, puts the youthful reader *au courant* with the story, and at the end of each chapter is a series of historical and explanatory notes. The book is well illustrated, and is in every way well adapted to encourage in the young a taste for reading."

SCOTSMAN.—"It makes a capital reading-book for 'English' classes."

WESTWARD HO! By CHARLES KINGSLEY. Abridged Edition for Schools. With Illustrations. 256 pages. Globe 8vo. 1s. 6d.

EDUCATIONAL NEWS.—"It is quite a pleasure to see that 'Westward Ho!' has been abridged for use in Schools. It is well and wisely done. . . . A thread of analysis conjoins all the parts, and yet we have in it all the finer vital passages which take hold on the mind and fill the imagination."

SCHOOLMASTER.—"It is a book that will please the children and help them to read."

SCHOLAR'S MAGAZINE.—"The lines have fallen upon the schoolboys and girls of the present day in very pleasant places indeed. Here is a modern classic, slightly abridged, beautifully printed, splendidly illustrated, neatly bound, and with just such helpful notes as will clear up those difficulties which a thoughtful upper standard child will be sure to find here and there in the text."

HEREWARD THE WAKE. By CHARLES KINGSLEY. Abridged Edition for Schools. With Illustrations. 256 pages. Globe 8vo. 1s. 6d.

EDUCATIONAL TIMES.—"The way in which this historical novel has been shortened so as to fit it for use as a School Reader reflects great credit on the unnamed editor. . . . The subject-matter is sure to interest boys and girls—an essential to the success of a reading book—and great discretion has been shown in the brief, clear explanation of difficult words, and difficult ones only."

EDUCATIONAL NEWS.—"Whoever the Editor may be, he has done a piece of good work for the moral and intellectual education of the young, of which teachers will approve."

ARITHMETIC.

ARITHMETIC FOR THE STANDARDS. By Rev. J. B. LOCK, M.A., and GEO. COLLAR, B.A., B.Sc.

Standard I.	. . .	2d.
Standard II.	. . .	2d.
Standard III.	. . .	2d.
Standard IV.	. . .	2d.
Standard V.	. . .	3d.
Standard VI.	. . .	3d.
Standard VII.	. . .	3d.

Answers to Standards I., II., III., IV., 3d. *each; Standards V., VI., VII.,* 4d. *each.*

SCHOOLMASTER.—"These Arithmetics are among the best in the market. We are struck with the thoroughness of the work of the compilers, especially in the upper Standards."

MACMILLAN AND CO., LONDON.

SCHEDULE I.—*Continued.*

MACMILLAN'S ARITHMETICAL TEST CARDS FOR THI STANDARDS.

Standards II., III., IV. and V., 60 cards in each packet, each card containin 16 Test Sums, and 2 Sets of Answers. Standard VI., 48 cards. Standard VII. 40 cards. 1s. 3d. each packet.

MACMILLAN'S MENTAL ARITHMETIC.

Standards I. and II., with Answers . . . . . 6d.
Standards III. and IV., with Answers . . . . 6d.
Standards V. and VI., with Answers . . . . 6d.

Also Standards I. to VI. separately, without Answers. 2d. each.

SCHEDULE II.

OBJECT LESSONS IN ELEMENTARY SCIENCE. By V. T MURCHÉ, Head Master of Boundary Lane Board School, Camberwell. Globe 8vc Part I., for Standards I. and II. 2s. 6d. Part II., for Standards III. an IV. 3s. Part III., for Standards V., VI., and VII. 3s. 6d.

SCHOOL BOARD CHRONICLE.—"Next to the practical knowledge an experience upon which they are based, the strong point of the lessons is their absolut thoroughness. Nothing is omitted that can be expressed in the written word. Wha to do and what to say are suggested concurrently, with clearness and precision, nc with the object of binding the experienced teacher to the smaller details as with tha of enabling him to rely very largely on the book, as affording sufficient guidance eve for pupil teachers, while leaving his own freedom unimpaired."

EDUCATIONAL NEWS.—"The London School Board recently issued a fu and thorough scheme of object teaching in elementary science for the guidance of thei staff. The headmaster of Boundary Lane Board School, Camberwell —whose lessor books on botany and physiology had won repute,—at once proceeded to provide fc each section of the school under his charge notes on lessons following the lines ind cated. From these the classes have been taught with a success so remarkable, tha the Vice-president of the Council of Education—Mr. A. H. D. Acland—at the sug gestion of H.M. Inspector, came to see the results, and recommended the publishin of the notes. They appear in three volumes—though each is complete in itself i matter and method, and, taken together, they form a condensed library of lessons i elementary science which only want a copious index for inter-reference to be perfec for their purpose. The book forms a manual of great value, and must greatly aid a who are anxious to train their pupils to know and rejoice in the world of wonders, t the perception of which science sharpens the sight of eye and mind. We commen it most heartily."

SCHEDULE III.

A TEXT-BOOK OF NEEDLEWORK, KNITTING, AND CUTTIN(OUT, WITH METHODS OF TEACHING. By ELIZABETH ROSEVEAR, Trainin College, Stockwell. With Illustrations. Third Edition. Crown 8vo. 6s.

NEEDLEWORK, KNITTING, AND CUTTING OUT FOR OLDEI GIRLS. By E. ROSEVEAR. Globe 8vo.

Standard IV. . . . . 6d.
Standard V. . . . . 8d.
Standards VI., VII., and Ex-VII. . . . 1s.

SCHOOL BOARD CHRONICLE.—"The lessons are addressed to the girl themselves, and great pains being taken to describe with absolute clearness an simplicity, it is thought that the older girls in these Standards will be able to prepar themselves, from the book, for practical home Needlework with little or no help in th shape of class lessons. The diagrams and illustrations are very numerous and helpful.

NEEDLEWORK: A Manual of Needlework, Knitting, and Cutting Out for Evening Continuation Schools. By ELIZABETH ROSEVEAR. Globe 8vo. 2!

MACMILLAN AND CO., LONDON.

www.ingramcontent.com/pod-product-compliance
Lightning Source LLC
Chambersburg PA
CBHW021806230426
43669CB00008B/646